Driving While Black
(By Association)

By J.J. Gathman

ISBN: 978-1-7371598-0-3

Edited by Robert M. Brent

Cover by York Griffith

Artwork by Jessie Rodriguez

THIS WORK DEPICTS ACTUAL EVENTS IN THE LIFE
OF THE AUTHOR. THE NAMES OF ALL INDIVIDUALS
HAVE BEEN CHANGED TO RESPECT THEIR PRIVACY.

CONTENTS

ACKNOWLEDGMENTS

Thanks to Jimison Coleman and Hassan "Cristos" Messiah for encouraging me to share my stories. Thank you Jade for all of your assistance.

1

BIG BLACK CADILLAC

In the late fall of '95, I was at a party with three of my friends. It was a Saturday night and we were four teenage boys looking to hopefully meet some girls. It was the kind of party where they charged $5 at the door. We were on the Near West Side of Chicago, in an area full of old warehouses and factories. There was a DJ spinning records, yes, actual vinyl records. In the 90s, DJs still had two turntables and a mixer. The big open warehouse space was full of young adults, just looking for somewhere to hang out. The crowd was made up of mostly Blacks and Latinos. I was one of the few White kids there. I was with my friends Marcel, Twan, and Brian, all of whom are Black. Marcel and Twan were friends of mine from high school. Brian grew up in the same neighborhood as Marcel and hung around with us sometimes.

We were all dressed in our freshest clothes, which in the mid 90s meant that everything we wore was at least one size too big. After we hung out for a while, just chilling and listening to the music, we ended up meeting some girls from the North Side. One of the girls gave Twan her digits on a scrap of paper, and based on his track record, we knew there was a very good chance that we would see those girls again. By that point it was getting late, and the festivities were dying down. Brian and I both had to work in the morning. It was time to bounce. I had recently saved up enough for a car, so we jumped in and headed home to Oak Park.

Marcel called shotgun, while Brian and Twan rode in the back. My car was a late-60s black Cadillac Eldorado. It was the size of a boat. My dad had advised against going for a cool old classic, saying it would be nothing but a pain in my ass, and he had been right. I ended up spending more on repairs than I did on the car itself.

As we passed Homan Avenue, going west on Chicago Avenue, we drove by an all-black Chevy Impala that was parked at a stop sign. Just after we passed, it pulled out and began to follow us for a couple of blocks. All of a sudden, red and blue lights were spinning in my rearview mirror amid the telltale blare of police sirens. I pulled over, my mind racing: I wasn't speeding or swerving; my license plate was legal and my taillights were working. I had never been in a car that was pulled over for no reason, and I couldn't figure out what I did wrong.

We sat there and waited, wondering what was going on. The Impala idled behind us, but no one was getting out. After about five long minutes, a blue and white Chicago police squad car pulled up and parked perpendicular to traffic. I wondered why they would do that. Both cars were sitting a noticeable distance from us, about thirty feet in front of my car, and thirty feet behind. The uniformed officers got out of the squad car. They took position behind their cruiser, guns drawn and pointed directly at my windshield. "Oh fuck, they ain't playing," Twan said, from the back seat.

Then we heard a loud voice blasting from a speaker. It was coming from the unmarked car behind us. "Lower all your windows and put your hands on the ceiling," the voice commanded.

We did what was asked of us. My hands pressed up to the ceiling of my car, I was trying not to breathe too heavily. There were guns pointed straight at us and I was afraid any movement could get us killed. Brian was in the back, quietly trying to keep everyone calm. "Just chill. Be easy. Don't give them a reason."

Without moving my head, my eyes darted between the guns in front of me and my side mirror. I started to see some movement. Two plain-clothes officers were slowly approaching from behind. They had their guns drawn and pointed at the car.

"Don't move or I'll fucking kill you," ordered the officer on my side of the car. He said it very matter-of-factly, like he actually meant it. My stomach jumped into my throat. Seconds later, I could feel the cold metal of his gun. He was pressing the barrel right into the bone behind my ear. "Slowly reach for the door handle and open it," he said. I carefully followed his instructions. "Now get out and put your hands on your head."

The officer was still pressing his gun to my head as I carefully got out of my car. He leaned me against the trunk, keeping his gun on me the whole time.

On the passenger side, the other plain-clothes cop aggressively pulled Marcel out of his seat. "Damn dude," Marcel yelled, "calm down!" The cop responded by slamming Marcel onto my trunk as hard as he could.

"Shut the fuck up!" he yelled. He was a huge guy, at least 6' 3", 250 pounds. Marcel couldn't have weighed more than 160 pounds back then.

Another marked car pulled up and parked behind the Impala. Two more uniformed officers emerged. They came over to get Brian and Twan out of the backseat.

The newly arrived uniformed cops were much calmer and cooler in their interactions with Brian and Twan. They began to search our pockets, socks, and shoes. "Where's the gun?" the cop who was frisking me asked. "Just tell me now. I'm going to be really fucking pissed if you lie to me."

I told him that there was no gun in the car.

"If I find a gun in this car, I'm going to fuck you up!" he warned.

The two cops who were pointing their guns at us from behind their car came over to assist. The plain-clothes officers began to search my trunk and then my car. The uniformed cops took our IDs and ran our information. None of us were on probation or had any outstanding warrants. The big guy was continuously talking shit to us as he searched the car. The longer he didn't find anything, the more agitated he became. Marcel kept asking them what we had done and was informed to "shut the fuck up" every time. I had a bunch of questions in my head, but I don't remember saying a word. I was just happy to no longer have a pistol jammed into my skull.

"You guys must have hid the gun under the backseat," the big cop said as he popped back out of my car. "I guess I'm gonna have to pull the fucking seat out!"

He spoke with a grin on his face. I watched through the rear window as he ripped the backseat out of my car. I can still see the crazed look in his eyes as he broke the framing and tore the original upholstery. He reminded me of a rampaging gorilla.

After destroying my seat without finding anything, he emerged from the car and headed straight over to Marcel. "Maybe we should search this fucking guy again," he said to the uniformed officers. The big cop slammed Marcel onto the trunk and aggressively patted him down. "He's probably got something stashed under his balls," he said, laughing as he spoke.

The officer then pulled Marcel off of the car and stood him upright. He yanked his pants down to the ground and made him spread his legs. The cop used the handle side of his flashlight to poke around Marcel's boxer shorts. Then he lowered the flashlight and smashed it up into Marcel's testicles. The pain was enough to drop Marcel straight to the pavement.

With Marcel lying on the street in his boxers, the two plain-clothes officers decided they were finished. "Get the fuck out of here," the big guy commanded. One of the uniformed cops gave us our IDs back. We jammed the bench seat back in as best as we could and got the fuck out of there.

On our way back down Chicago Avenue. We began to let out our

4

frustration. Twan and Brian were in the backseat, questioning how tough those cops would be without their guns. Marcel just stared out the window. I don't remember him saying a thing.

After dropping everyone off, I headed home, and I remember feeling very relieved upon parking my car and hopping out. It felt like the car was a dangerous place, and I just wanted to get inside and lock the deadbolt behind me. I tried to sleep, but sleep was not coming easy—I had so much adrenaline pumping through me.

I went down to my basement to smoke a cigarette (still a common habit in the 90s). I just sat there smoking, as everything that happened replayed itself over and over in my head. I thought of all those guns pointed at us, and of how one false move could have ended in a bloodbath. Everything raced through my mind at once. At that point in life, I don't think I really understood what I was feeling, I was mad about a bunch of things. Of all the stuff that went down, I was mostly pissed about how they fucked up my car. As a teenager, money was harder to come by, and I had worked after school and on weekends to pay for that car. They damaged the original parts of a classic car, and the whole ordeal was unprovoked. That was the part I really couldn't understand.

Marcel, Twan, and I hung out a few days later. We hadn't really talked about the prior Saturday night yet. We were chilling after school in Bobby's basement. Bobby was a kid we went to high school with, but I wouldn't exactly call him a friend. His mom was never home, so his place was always available for hanging out. Twan was still really angry about what happened. He wanted to go one-on-one with that big detective. I'm sure he wouldn't have had a prayer in a fight with that giant cop, but I understood that he just wanted some form of payback.

Bobby told us that we needed to sue the Police Department. He bragged about knowing a powerful lawyer. The thought had crossed my mind, but I just couldn't imagine how we could win that case. It was very frustrating for us. All we were left with was a desire to make them pay for what they did, but we had no actual recourse. For many teenage males, the natural instinct is to want to find the guys and fight them. That was definitely not an option when dealing with the police.

Filing a lawsuit was an option, but how could we prove any of it? We had the right as Americans to sue the police, but it felt like a pretty hollow right, especially when they acted so aggressively. They forced our adrenaline to go way up, and our ability to remember exact details became very difficult. They put us in a position where we didn't dare make eye contact with them. I don't think I could have picked any of those cops out of a lineup, except maybe the big guy. They left me with a fuzzy head and all I wanted to do was get as far away from them as possible.

Marcel wasn't that interested in talking about Saturday night. He just said that the police are "psychos and there's nothing you can do about it." I figured he was pretty embarrassed about what they did to him. I can still remember the look on his face when he was standing there in his boxers on Chicago Ave. It was a chilly night, somewhere around forty degrees outside. He was shaking from being cold. People were staring at him, as they walked by. Cars after car passed by, as he stood there on display. Chicago Avenue is a busy city street. It's lined with storefronts and apartments. The police conducted what should have been a private search in a very public place, except that it was actually an illegal and unprovoked search. Marcel had a detective poking a flashlight under his balls, with his pants around his ankles. I completely understood his lack of words.

I don't think we ever discussed that night again. I have no recollection of talking about it with Brian. I tried to shake the incident off, but I remained pretty angry about it. I quickly developed a personal rivalry with the police. Being in a store, at the same time as a cop, made me uncomfortable. I found myself talking shit every time I saw a police car pass by.

I realize now that I was angry because the police took something from me. Growing up, I often heard how lucky I was to be American. It was presented to me as a privilege that I was supposed to be kind of guilty about. My biggest reason to be a proud American had always been the fact that I had individual rights. That night, I learned how easily some cops could take those perceived rights away from me. Some teenagers are cynical because they are teenagers and its part of the deal. I became a true cynic because the police made one.

That Saturday night wasn't my first interaction with the police, but any previous times I dealt with them, they had treated us like kids, whether I was out past curfew or loitering in a park after it was closed. They had given us warnings and told us to go home. But this time, those officers put us in a position that made us completely helpless. It's not like we could have called the police on the police. From the beginning, they took one hundred percent of the power. We had to do what they said, at gunpoint. They never told us why they pulled us over. They never asked me if they could search my car or trunk. When we had guns pointed at us and every question we asked was answered with "shut the fuck up," we really had no rights. Back then, very few people carried cell phones and the cell phones from that era did not have cameras. The police didn't have body cameras. They operated without any fear of facing consequences for their actions. On top of everything, I couldn't understand why none of the cops were Black when we were in the 11th District, an almost entirely Black section of Chicago.

I learned that there had been another major factor in our incident with the police that I was unaware of. A few months later, I became friends with an older dude. He had recently moved to my neighborhood. He was in his early forties, a Black guy, who everyone called "Papa Foe." He was from West Garfield Park, an extremely rough neighborhood. We became cool very quickly. He was the type to tell stories and share his wisdom. Papa Foe had lived a hard life. He lost a lot of family and friends to murder. Somehow, he still had a very even keeled and spiritual view of life.

He loved my old Cadillac; he was a kid when that car rolled off the assembly line, but one of the first things he ever told me was, "You gotta get rid of that ride."

"When the police see your car," Papa Foe told me, "all they see is a big Black gangster coming down the street." He explained how the police assume race when they see cars. "You might as well be Black, if you gonna drive this car," he said. I bought the car because I thought it was cool and

I could afford it. I never gave it much thought. Papa Foe's insight brought my mind back to that night on Chicago Avenue. Everything made more sense to me. I was sure that the police had made their minds up the second they saw my big black Cadillac coming down the street. We were probably targeted before they could even see who was in the car.

2

ABC:

ANOTHER BULLSHIT CASE

It was February of 1996, a few months after the incident on Chicago Avenue. I was out with some friends on another Saturday night. Twan's mom let him borrow her car, which was a rare event. He had picked me up from my house, but we had no plans. Twan was just happy to have a car. I had just gotten off work and I was pretty tired, so I wasn't looking to do anything major. At that age, I never wasted an opportunity to go out on the weekend. We rode around aimlessly for a while and ended up stopping to get something to eat at a gyros joint. While we were eating, some kids we knew came through the door. Ant and Tez had walked up there from Ant's apartment. They ordered some food and sat with us.

Tez was good friends with Ant, who lived a few blocks from me and went to school with us. Tez lived down on the South Side, but I had been over to his place with Ant several times, so I knew him pretty well. He was definitely a little man with a big mouth. Twan didn't like him very much, but because he was friends with Ant, we ended up hanging out with him more often than we would've preferred.

After we ate, we all got in Twan's car and drove to Ant's girlfriend's place, where she was hanging out with a couple of her friends. After chilling there for a while, my pager started to vibrate. It was my boy "Carlito" (his friends called him "Lito"), a Mexican kid who Ant and I were friends with. He was asking if we wanted to come by, and he owed me $20, a decent amount of money back then. He lived in Cicero, which was only a short drive from us, so Twan agreed to give me a ride. I called Lito and let him know we were coming over.

The four of us jumped in the car and headed to Lito's crib. As we headed south, down Central Avenue, Twan was having second thoughts. The Cicero police are known to be corrupt and had a reputation for messing with Black people. Tez jumped into the conversation. "I don't know man, maybe you could drop me off at that corner store we just passed," he said. "You could pick me up on the way back." Tez had never spent any time around Mexican people and he was nervous about going into Lito's neighborhood. For different reasons, both Tez and Twan were having reservations. I was trying to convince them that it was cool and nothing bad was going to happen.

We were about to cross Roosevelt Road, where Chicago ended and Cicero began. Twan pulled into a parking lot and argued with me for a minute. I started thinking that if we did have an issue with the police, then everyone would blame me.

"Fuck it, then!" I said. "Let's just turn around." I knew that I could get up with Lito anytime. It wasn't worth the drama.

We pulled out of the parking lot and turned north on Central Ave. Before we knew it, red and blue lights were flashing behind us. None of us ever saw a cop car. It felt like they appeared out of thin air. "Here we go again," I said to Twan.

I was feeling very differently that time around. I had some anger in me from our last encounter with the police. I was more mentally prepared than before. I felt ready for whatever was coming next.

I looked in the side mirror and saw a blue and white Chicago police car behind us. Again, they just sat there. I realized that this is how the Chicago Police operated. They must have been waiting for backup. Tez was panicking behind me, in the backseat. Twan was getting really irritated with him.

"Shut the fuck up man!" Twan told Tez.

"That shit's not helping, dude." I agreed with Twan. "Stop acting like a little kid," I told him.

Ant was able to get him to calm down, to some degree. While we were sitting there waiting, the reality of the situation hit me. We were mysteriously getting pulled over and the racial makeup of the car was most likely the cause.

A few minutes later, another marked police car pulled up. They parked right in front of Twan's car, boxing us in. Two uniformed cops emerged from the car behind us. One officer was a young White male. The other officer was a White female, around forty years old. The female officer went to Twan's window as the male cop stood on my side. He instructed me to put my hands on the dashboard. He told Tez and Ant to put their hands on their heads. The female cop had her gun out, but she had it lowered.

"Slowly get your license out of your pocket," she told Twan. He handed her his license. Next, she asked for the car's registration. Twan apparently reached for the glove compartment too quickly, because she pointed her gun at him and told him to "slow down!"

The two cops in the other car came over. They were both White males, probably in their thirties. The female officer handed Twan's license and registration to one of them. He went back to his car and ran the information. Twan and I were removed from the car and placed with our hands on the trunk. The officers that pulled us over patted us down. Tez and Ant remained in the backseat, with their hands on their heads.

The young male cop was frisking me. "So were you sniffing some dope?" he asked. On the West Side of Chicago, 'dope' always means heroin. The West Side is notorious for selling a form of China White heroin that can be snorted up the nose.

"What are you talking about?" I replied. "We were just turning around dude!"

"Show some fucking respect or this is going to go really bad for you!" The female cop jumped in.

"This guy is disrespecting me," I piped back. "He's acting like I'm a dopehead or something!"

"Cuff him!" She commanded. The young guy drove my head into the trunk with his elbow. He leaned all of his weight onto me. He aggressively handcuffed me, intentionally over-tightening them. I couldn't feel my fingertips after a few minutes.

The cop who was running Twan's info returned. "Everything is clean," he said. The female cop instructed the other officers to pull Ant and Tez out of the backseat. They searched all of us and found nothing illegal.

"What did we do?" Twan asked them a couple of times. It was like he wasn't even speaking. They just ignored the question. The female cop searched the car and the trunk, while one of the other officers ran the rest of our IDs.

Tez was pleading. "I don't want to go to jail," he repeatedly told them.

"This is some bullshit man," Twan mumbling.

"What did you say?" the female officer asked him.

"Nothing, I didn't say nothing," he responded. She pulled her flashlight out. "No, tell me what you said," she demanded. "Come on, tell me what you fucking said!" She swung the flashlight and hit him across the back. Twan laughed a little, so she hit him again. The second time, Twan grimaced in pain. The flashlight caught him right on the neck. "Okay, now you're going to jail," she informed him. She cuffed him and put him in the back of her car.

"You know what? They're all going to jail," she told the other cops. "Let's go."

The backup officers cuffed Ant and Tez. Tez was still begging as they put them in the back of their car. The female officer started searching around the parking lot. I couldn't figure what she was looking for. She came back to her car, where I was now in the backseat with Twan. "So you guys did that graffiti, huh?" she questioned. She was pointing to some really old tags on the wall of a factory.

"What are you talking about?" Twan asked. I didn't say a word, because I could tell that there was no point. She wasn't asking a question; she was making a declaration. She got behind the wheel and we drove away. "What about my car?" Twan asked. The officers didn't reply. They left his mother's car sitting there unlocked with the windows rolled down.

We arrived at the Austin Precinct of the Chicago Police Department, the 15th District. They brought us in and sat us on a bench. They started their paperwork, which took forever. Nowadays our phones are better computers than the ones they were using back then. The female officer took me to her desk because I had recently turned eighteen years old, so I was processed separately. It was the last I saw of the others that night.

Twan and Ant were both seventeen, and Tez was fifteen. Being processed as minors meant they needed a guardian to come and pick them up. This was really bad news for Tez's mom. She had to come all the way from the South Side, about a hundred blocks away. She ended up taking two L trains and a bus to get there. Twan's mom had to take a cab, because her car was sitting on Central Avenue.

I sat there for about thirty minutes, as the cop took her time processing me. After she finished all of my paperwork, she read me my charges. I was charged with three misdemeanors. Criminal trespass to property, disorderly conduct, and criminal defacement of property. I was charged as though we vandalized that factory. I just shook my head and didn't say a thing.

She escorted me to the lockup entrance. She turned a key to open a huge metal door. There, two officers conducted another search on me. They took the shoelaces out of my shoes and removed everything from my pockets. They put it all into a plastic bag and sealed it. As I was waiting, I looked around. It was Saturday night and the place was packed already. Every cell I could see was full. With so many bodies in one space, it felt like a hundred degrees in there. I was in the old Austin Precinct building. The city built a big new precinct about ten years later. The old precinct was built in 1917, and by the 1990s, it was a dump.

"You get one phone call and you should use it now," they informed me. The officer pointed to a payphone on the wall. I made a collect phone call to my house. My dad answered. It sounded like he had been sleeping. I told him where I was and all he said was, "okay." I told him that I would wait it out. I didn't want him or my mom to come bail me out. I figured they would be less mad if I had to sit in there awhile.

One of the officers walked me all the way to the back, past a bunch of cells. There was 100% Black occupancy in there until I showed up. He placed me in a small cell with three other guys. Two of them were in their early twenties. The other guy was in his thirties. He was out cold on one of the two, extremely uncomfortable benches. The other two guys were sitting and talking on the opposite bench. There was a small unoccupied space at the end of the bench where the older guy was sleeping.

"What up jo?" one of the guys said. The other guy nodded his head to me. "Jo" is a common slang term in Chicago, the equivalent of "bro" or "dude."

I nodded my head in response. I squeezed into the only available spot, right next to the seatless toilet. The two guys sitting across from me went back to their conversation. I got the impression that they might have known each other. I had never been locked up before, so I wasn't sure what to expect. I wasn't in any old jail: I was in the 15th District, one of the highest crime districts in all of Chicago. I was legally an adult for a matter of weeks. The word 'adult' was becoming very real to me. That was my first time in jail and I was thrown right into the major leagues.

The place was buzzing. All of the conversations coming from the other cells were bouncing off of the concrete walls. Some guys were yelling to dudes they knew in other cells. The guy sleeping next to me was snoring like a chainsaw. I could only assume that he was drunk. I couldn't imagine any other way that someone could sleep so well on a metal bench. I started to relax, but I wasn't sure if I should be nervous or not. I was definitely the odd man out in terms of race. I didn't know if that was going to be a factor. All I could think while sitting there was, so far so good.

About thirty minutes later, one of the officers shouted my name. He was trying to locate the cell I was in. I hopped up and waved my hand through the bars. I was excited. I figured that they were going to let me go to make some space. The officer opened the cell door and escorted me back to the room, where they searched me. He pointed to a chair and told me to "Take a seat."

I sat there for at least five minutes. I couldn't figure out why they had me sitting in that chair. The female officer, who arrested me, entered the room. She was pissed.

"Where is my fucking badge?" she yelled.

"What do you mean?" I replied.

"My badge, my badge is missing! It was on my desk and now it's gone. What the fuck did you do with my badge?" she screamed, as she got into my face. "You must have hid it or something."

"I don't know what you're talking about," I answered. "I didn't touch your badge, I swear."

"You little fucking shit," she shouted, as she punched me in the chest. I insisted that I didn't know what she was talking about. "You're fucked," she informed me, as she punched me in the chest again. That time, she really put everything she had into it, almost knocking the wind out of me. "Alright, get him out of here," she commanded. She was still very angry as she left the room.

One of the lockup officers brought me back to my cell. "Man, you fucked up!" He told me. "It looks like you're going to The County in the morning." I was really confused. I had no idea what she was talking about. I didn't remember even seeing her badge on the desk. I will admit, I was getting pretty nervous at that point. I did not want to go to Cook County Jail. I had heard my whole life how it was the worst jail in America. I knew for a fact that inmates agreed to terrible deals with the prosecutors just to get out of there. They would happily go to prison just to not be in The County any longer.

When I was placed back in the cell, the guys sitting on the bench were smiling. "Ayy, you really pissed them off jo!" one of them said. "What the fuck you do?"

"They're tripping!" I replied. "I didn't do shit." He laughed and then stood up on the bench. "Yeah man, they be on some bullshit!" he shouted.

He made sure the officers up front could hear him. That woke up the older guy. He looked around and saw me sitting in the corner. "My bad, here man," he said as he pulled his legs up. He realized that he was taking up most of the bench. I appreciated the gesture and felt some camaraderie.

I settled into a slightly more comfortable position and tried to sleep. About thirty minutes later, they brought in another guy. He was a young Black kid. He didn't look old enough to even be in there. Like myself, I assumed that he must have just turned eighteen. "Damn man," he shouted, "this place is packed like a motherfucker!" The two guys across from me scooted over to give him room to sit.

"Ayy, I snuck some squares in," the new kid whispered ("squares" is a common term in Chicago for cigarettes). He pulled four Newports out of his shoe. "Anyone in here got a lighter?" he asked. None of us had snuck a lighter in. "Who's got a lighter in this joint?" he shouted to the other cells. "I got you," some dude we couldn't see replied, "but you better send it back." The lighter passed through some other cells, on its way to us.

"Man jo, I'm so fucking hungry!" the new kid looked at me and said, "I'll trade you one of these squares for your sandwich." One of the officers had just announced that they were bringing us bologna sandwiches soon.

I had no appetite. I was too stressed to eat anything. I happily agreed to this transaction. He made the same deal with one of the other guys and kept two cigarettes for himself. We lit up our squares and sent the lighter back.

"Appreciated," the young dude yelled to the anonymous lender of the lighter.

I had smelled cigarette smoke the entire time I was in there. We weren't technically allowed to smoke, but the officers weren't enforcing the rule. Looking back, I assume, the officers viewed smoking as a type of pacifier. Letting us smoke the smuggled cigarettes helped keep some peace. I sat back and milked that Newport for everything it was worth, trying to kill as much time as possible.

About an hour later, they started releasing some of the guys in there. The older dude, who was sleeping the whole time, got his name called. That freed up some room in our tiny cell. "The bus for The County will be here in an hour," an officer announced. That information made my stomach turn a little. The thought of going to The County was bad, but it seemed worse knowing I hadn't even broken any laws.

Another thirty minutes had passed before I heard one of the officers shouting for me. I hoped it wouldn't be like the last time they had called my name. After a few more minutes, one of the officers appeared, unlocked the door, and walked me out of my cell toward the main entrance.

"You're going home," he said. I figured that the female officer had found her badge and her issues with me were squashed. "Go up front and get your stuff," he instructed, as they opened up the big metal door. Once at the front desk, they gave me the plastic bag with my belongings, and had me sign an I-bond. This meant that I wouldn't have to pay anything unless I missed my court date, in which case I would owe $500.

I walked out of the police station and stood there on the sidewalk for a minute. I was happy to breathe the cold air as I took in the view of freedom. Early on a Sunday morning, a normally bustling hood was very calm. The sun was just breaking over the skyscrapers to the east. I hadn't been paying any attention to time, but I spent around seven hours in there. I sat on the curb and laced my shoes back up. While sitting there, I realized that the idea of freedom really depended on your situation. The word "freedom" became much more literal to me.

Home was only twelve blocks away, so I had an easy enough walk ahead of me. I took my time. Walking felt good after being jammed up for that long. I wasn't really looking forward to talking to my parents. I didn't know if they would believe my story. I went through it in my head and it sounded like bullshit. When I got to my house, my mom was awake and my dad was still sleeping. I told her that we didn't do anything. I don't know if she believed me. She told me to get something to eat and we could talk about it later. I still didn't have an appetite, so I took a shower and got into my bed.

Again, I couldn't fall asleep. I had mixed feelings. I was happy to be out of jail, but I was thinking about all those dudes that were on their way to The County. I wondered how many of them were actually guilty of anything. I felt grateful to be free, but my anger toward the police was cemented.

My parents didn't make a big deal about the situation. They were both born and raised in Chicago and weren't naive to police corruption. My dad treated my arrest as something I just had to deal with. Basically, handle the situation and move on. He knew a lawyer that he could get some free advice from. He told me that he would give him a call sometime that week. I had a court date scheduled about six weeks from then.

On that Monday, I got up with Ant and Twan after school. We typically met up with each other on a corner across from our high school. A lot of kids that I knew would congregate on that corner when school let out. Our high school had over 3,500 students. Kids could go a whole day and only see their friends in passing. The three of us plus Marcel made our way to Ant's apartment. We hung out on the front steps for a while. It was cold outside, but at that age we didn't care. We would rather be out in the cold than sitting around at home.

Both Ant and Twan had been chewed out thoroughly after getting arrested. The two of them and Tez were scheduled to go to juvenile court together. Ant was slightly worried about it, because he had some prior juvenile offenses. On the other hand, he didn't think very far into the future, so most things didn't bother him much. He was mad that the police set us up, but it was already in the past for him.

Twan was fuming though. I could see something building up inside of him. His personality was changing. He always had righteous ideas and goals for his future. After our encounter with the police, a few months earlier, he started to carry himself with more visible anger. On top of having to go to court on bogus charges, Twan figured his mom wasn't going to let him borrow her car for a long time. Marcel had nothing good to say about the police, but he was happy that he wasn't with us that night.

When my court date arrived, I showed up wearing a tie. I really didn't want to wear that tie. I felt like I was kissing somebody's ass or something. My dad told me how the judge would view me differently if I made the effort. I was at Flournoy Street and Kenzie Avenue, a rundown old courthouse in the heart of the West Side.

When the bailiff called my name, I went before the judge. He asked about my legal defense and I requested a court-appointed attorney. The judge granted me a public defender, because I did not earn much money working part-time. The lawyer that my dad had spoken with advised me to take that route. I could switch lawyers later if I needed to.

I was back in court, a few weeks later. I got there thirty minutes early, in order to meet with my court-appointed attorney. My lawyer was a man in his fifties and was visibly worn down. I assumed his job was exhausting. He wanted to hear what the judge had to say and go from there, since I had no prior convictions. He had to meet with more people, so I only had a few minutes of his time.

I took a seat in the courtroom and waited for the judge to enter. Soon after court was in session the female officer who had arrested me came walking in. My chest tightened up a little. I didn't think she was going to show up. She knew I didn't do anything. I figured she was just going to let it go. I went before the judge and the prosecutor approached the bench.

The prosecutor informed the judge that he was intending to prosecute me on all charges. The judge told me to talk to my lawyer and he would call us back to the bench later. I had to decide if I was going to claim my innocence. Pleading not guilty meant I would go to trial.

"I'll talk with the prosecutor and see what I can do," my lawyer told me. I waited in the courtroom until my public defender came and got me. We went out front and talked. "The prosecutor wants you to do fifty hours of community service," he told me. "I was able to talk him down to thirty hours, because you have no criminal history." He advised me to plead guilty and take the deal. "There's no way we'll do better at trial," he said.

"I need a minute to think about it," I replied. He acted like the deal on the table might expire, so I needed to be timely in my decision making.

I was conflicted. I didn't want to plead guilty to something I didn't do. I wasn't looking forward to doing thirty hours of community service, when the police were the only people guilty of something. I was sure that my lawyer would not be happy if I chose to go to trial. I had no faith that this guy would represent me very well. After I thought about it, I decided to plead not guilty and hire a new lawyer. When the judge called me back up, I informed him of my decision. I was given a new court date.

At home, my dad had more secondhand advice for me. "You need to find a lawyer that has a lot of cases in that courthouse," he told me. "Lawyers like to work the same courthouses, because they develop relationships with the judges and the prosecutors." He wanted me to take a day off of school and sit in the courtroom. That way I could find a lawyer who had multiple clients that day. Later that week, my mom and I spent half of a day observing the court.

One lawyer really stood out. He was in and out of the courtroom, walking and talking with authority. We caught up with him outside, after court was adjourned for the day. He was a middle-aged White guy that reeked of confidence. He spoke quickly, with a thick Chicago accent. He agreed to take my case and he gave me his card. He wanted me to call him in a couple of days so we could discuss the details.

When I talked to him on the phone, he had me go over everything that happened that night. When I was finished, he bluntly asked me, "Did you do it?"

"All we did was turn around in a parking lot," I told him.

"That's good, that means that they don't have any evidence against you," he said. "It's a lot easier for me to defend innocent people. You should be alright and we'll go to trial, if we need to." He shared some wisdom with me which opened my eyes. "If we go to trial," he said, "we'll have a bench trial. It's easier to put it into the hands of the judge. These judges are swamped with garbage cases. The police are constantly bringing people to court on petty charges with little to no evidence. This pisses the judges off. With a case like yours, the judge is most likely going to lean your way. So there's no point in dealing with a jury."

I was surprised to hear that. I didn't know that some judges were skeptical of the police. I always thought a jury of your peers was the way to go. I thought judges were grumpy old people, who viewed every defendant as a criminal. My lawyer made me realize that judges are people who have their own opinions. I understand now that judges can be very different depending on the city, county, or state. I do realize that 'The Chicago Way' is often unique. There are a lot of places where the judges will typically side with the police, even with a lack of evidence.

My lawyer really appeared to know what he was talking about. I was happy to hear everything that he had to say, and I felt encouraged to fight the case. The cost of his services was $600. It sounded like a lot of money to me, but I felt like it was worth it. I didn't want to have those petty convictions on my record. In my mind, the police could haul me to jail again for no reason. If that were to happen, I would be facing the court with a record and the prosecutor would be more aggressive.

The evening before my court date, my lawyer gave me a call. He told me to be at the courthouse early. I was going to be one of the first defendants of the day. My lawyer had to be somewhere else later that morning. He was able to bump me to the front of line. This added to my confidence in him. I knew he must have had some clout in that courthouse.

I got to court early that morning. I went full-blown preppy guy, in terms of my clothes. I was wearing some khaki pants, a blue dress shirt, and a red tie. I looked like I was running for congress.

My lawyer arrived and we took a seat in the courthouse. Just like he said, I was the second person called to the bench. I looked around the courtroom and I didn't see any police officers that I recognized. That was a good sign. The prosecutor looked at his file and then approached the bench. "A.B.C.," he mumbled to the judge. The judge nodded his head. "Another bullshit case," he said to himself, under his breath. "Dismissed!" he proclaimed, in a singsong tone, and banged his gavel.

We walked out of the courtroom and I was trying not to grin, both because I was pleased with the result, and because there was something humorous about the interaction I had just witnessed. I didn't want to seem too happy in front of the other defendants, though. I knew that some of them were going to get some bad news that day. I was a little stunned by what had just happened. We definitely found the right lawyer. He was able to pull some strings or something. I thanked him for everything. He patted me on the back, shook my hand, and he was out of there. I couldn't believe it was over, just like that.

I was happy to be done with the whole thing, but it felt bittersweet. I felt like I had won, but I knew in the big picture I had lost. Time, money, and seven hours of my freedom. Those were all losses. I thought about all of the people who didn't have the money to fight for their freedom. I knew I was lucky to get good advice and that other people didn't necessarily have those avenues to work with. The whole thing just made me wonder, why does our society handle freedom this way? How could something we hold so high be reduced to connections and dollars?

The irony of the night we got arrested was not lost on me. Twan turned the car around to avoid crossing into Cicero. The odds were, we wouldn't have gotten pulled over or arrested if we'd just stayed the course. Turning around ended up being the wrong decision. Life can be random like that. It's even more random when you factor in aggressive police officers.

3

COPS & ROBBERS

On a hot summer day, back in '97, I was hanging out with Ant at his girlfriend's house. The heat and the humidity were unbearable. The news had issued a 'smog warning' and told people not to spend too much time outside. Ant's girlfriend, Nia, was seven months pregnant with Ant's son, and was feeling sick from the conditions. Ant and Nia were excited to have a child on the way, but of course they were nervous. They were both teenagers, so they knew that it was going to be challenging. Ant was working 'the line' in a restaurant that summer. He was trying to save as much money as possible before Nia gave birth. Ant had just gotten off of work. He was in the kitchen all day and was clearly overheated.

We were sitting on the front steps, because they didn't have air-conditioning, and it was even hotter inside Nia's house. Nia's mom was from Belize and she would say, "You think this is hot? This ain't nothing." Both Ant and Nia looked like they were going to faint. We needed some relief, so we got in my car and headed for the lakefront.

We went to "the rocks" at Diversey Harbor, on the North Side. It's a spot on Lake Michigan where a lot of teenagers would hang out. In the summer, people went to the lake just to cool off. The breeze coming off of the freshwater was like free air conditioning. We just chilled there for hours, cooling off and taking in the view. More and more people were flocking to the lakefront as the day wore on.

The sun was setting and it started to feel like a party was breaking out. Music was blasting out of boomboxes, and some people had brought food and beverages with them. I met a girl who was pretty cool, and she invited us to join in with her family and friends. We were having a good time, but Nia was starting to get tired. I didn't really want to leave, but I understood that she needed to get home. I could only imagine how it felt to be pregnant on a blazing hot day. I gave the girl my pager number and we headed home.

On our way back, I received a page from a number that I didn't recognize. I was hoping that it was the girl who I had just met, but that seemed too quick. I pulled over at a liquor store and used a payphone. It was Marcel. He was at his cousin's place, and he wanted to go out and do something that night. His cousin lived near Douglas Park, which was on our way back to Nia's. We pulled up, right off of Grenshaw Street and Springfield Ave. There were people everywhere. It seemed like the whole neighborhood was outside. The sun was down and the heat was letting up. There was a lot of energy in the air and I could tell it was going to be a lively night.

Marcel was hanging out with a bunch of people in front of his cousin's building. He wasn't ready to leave yet, so we parked the car and joined them. When we were getting ready to bounce, a car came creeping out of the alley and turned onto the block. The car didn't have its headlights on, and that got everyone's attention. Ant grabbed Nia and led her away from the group.

"Who that? Who that?" Marcel's cousin started yelling. I was getting ready to start ducking. The car pulled up and it was the police. A couple of detectives were inching down the block in an unmarked car. That was the only time in my life that I was happy to see the police.

They stopped right in front of us and just sat there grinning. They didn't say a word, but they didn't have to. They accomplished their goal, whatever it was. They had put everyone in a panic and they thought it was funny. Throughout my life I've seen the police use this move many times. Every time I had the same feeling. It felt like some predators were out looking for their prey. They were sliding through alleys and blocks, with their lights off, hoping to find something they could feast on.

"We getting up out of here!" Marcel declared. We said our goodbyes and we took off. Marcel took shotgun and Ant jumped in the backseat with Nia. We watched the detective's car go east, so we headed north up Springfield Ave. We only got a few blocks up the street before we saw another unmarked car. They were sitting at a stop sign. Unmarked cars are easier to spot from behind, because all of their gear is visible through the back window. Also, they're usually specific makes and models. In that era, the detectives typically drove Ford Crown Victorias or Chevy Impalas.

I was hoping that it wasn't the same cops that we had just encountered. Those two looked hungry for some action. As we pulled around the dark gray "Crown Vic," I took a quick glance. I was relieved to see a couple of different faces. They were both ethnic looking White guys. I made sure to make a full stop behind the line. I didn't want to give them anything easy.

"Man, there are a lot of cops out here tonight!" Marcel laughed and said, "We need to get the fuck off these streets as soon as possible."

We were almost halfway down the block when I saw them pull off of the curb in my rearview mirror. "They on us man," Marcel informed everyone. "They on us!" We started to get nervous. The squad car hung behind us and took a left turn with me. Right then, they flicked their lights on. "What the fuck?" I proclaimed. "I've gotta sell this car or something!"

I pulled over to the curb and prepared myself for some bullshit. I figured they would sit there and wait for some backup, but they just hopped right out of their car. One cop covered the passenger side and the other guy came straight to my window. The detective on Marcel and Nia's side looked like he was in his thirties. The cop at my window was older, probably in his late forties.

They carried themselves like some gangsters. They were both rocking bulletproof vests, with their badges dangling from chains around their necks. The older detective had a cigarette tucked behind his ear, while the younger guy kept adjusting his badge like it was a diamond-encrusted medallion.

"What's up buddy?" the older guy asked me, in a thick Chicago accent, "How ya doing?" I was a little thrown off by his approach. "I'm good, officer," I replied. I had come to realize that they liked to be called "officer." It was like bowing down a little, without kissing their asses completely.

"Why don't all you guys step out of the car, so we can have a chat?" the older detective asked. He wasn't asking though. He was commanding us. We got out of the car and they separated us into pairs. The younger cop brought Ant and Nia over to their car. The older detective placed Marcel and I, with our hands on the hood of my car. "So did you score some dope?" he asked as he searched me. The question irritated me. I thought to myself, "Again with the heroin questions! Why do the police keep thinking that I'm a dope fiend?"

"Do I look like a dopehead or something?" I fired back, "Why would you just assume that?" He started laughing. Which made me more irritated. "What does a dopehead look like?" he asked me.

"Not like me!" I told him. "Look at my clothes. Look at my shoes."

"Oh yeah, those are nice." he laughed again and asked, "What kinda shoes are those?"

"They're some Air Maxes," I replied. "They're limited editions." I wasn't normally the type to talk about my clothes, but I was trying to make a point. I was wearing brand new shoes and my clothes were fresh and clean. In my mind, this did not fit the description of a dopehead.

"Hey, we've got a big shot over here," he shouted to the other detective. "His shoes are limited editions!" The younger guy laughed.

"Look, I'm just saying," I interjected, "I don't do dope."

26

"That's good," he said, "it's a bad habit." He finished up his search of me and found nothing illegal.

The younger detective was patting Nia down on the unmarked car. "This is an illegal search," she told him. "You have no right to search me! We didn't do nothing."

"Calm down or I'm gonna cuff you," he warned her.

"What are your names?" She shouted back, "I'm going to need to know your name officer." He didn't answer the question. Instead, he cuffed Nia and sat her on the curb.

She kept talking and that angered the older cop. "Stay right here and don't even think about running," he told Marcel and me. "I'll fucking shoot both of ya!" He went over to Nia and asked her, "Do you want to go to jail?"

"How can you treat a pregnant girl like this?" She replied.

"You won't be the only pregnant girl in jail tonight, so shut the fuck up!" he responded.

"You don't need to speak to me like that!" Nia told him. "Look at me, I'm seven months pregnant."

He laughed at her.

"Yeah and I bet you don't even know who the dad is," he said.

"Come on man! That's my son she's carrying," Ant shouted, jumping into the conversation. "What the fuck dude?"

The younger detective responded by slamming him into their car. "Shut your fucking mouth or you can go to jail too," he warned him.

"I'd get one of those DNA tests if I were you," the older guy told Ant, "with these types of girls, you never know."

"What do you mean 'these types of girls?'" Nia took offense.

"Listen, if I hear another word out of your big mouth," the older detective said, "you're going to jail. Don't fucking test me!" Nia could see that he was dead serious and she didn't say another word.

The older detective returned to my car and searched Marcel. He patted Marcel down thoroughly. He didn't find anything. "Take off your shoes," he instructed both of us. After inspecting my shoes, he let me put them back on. He pulled the insoles out of Marcel's shoes. "Look what we've got here!" he exclaimed. He pulled out a few small bags of marijuana. He opened one of the bags and smelled it. "Oh fuck, this is some good shit," he whispered.

His demeanor instantly changed. He lit up his cigarette and appeared to be excited by this discovery. At that point he began to speak quietly. "You know I can bring you in for distribution, right?" he asked Marcel. "You've got multiple bags on you. Have you been out here selling weed?"

"No, I bought those for myself," Marcel answered. "I'm being one hundred percent real with you. That ain't nothing but a few blunts right there."

"It doesn't matter how much it is," the detective said. "It's bagged up for distribution, and would you look at that? We just happen to be next to a park." He pointed to a small public playground.

"That's another charge right there." He grinned as he spoke. "It looks like you've got some shitty luck."

I wasn't aware of this at that time, but the possession of drugs with an intent to distribute within 1,500 feet of a school, park, or church is a separate charge.

"Aww man, please! Please don't do me like that," Marcel begged, "We was just driving home. I'm not trying to go to jail tonight. Please man!" I had never heard Marcel talk that way before. He wasn't the type to lower himself to anyone, but he knew that there was a case adding up against him.

Right then and there, I saw how the police could take away the spirit of the law and replace it with cold and calculated charges. The detective knew Marcel wasn't selling that marijuana. The police hold the power to manipulate the law that way. The officer could charge him with a small possession, or he could charge him as though he were selling drugs near a playground. One would have likely led to a slap on the wrist and the other could have resulted in real jail time.

"Okay listen, maybe we can figure something out," the detective replied. "We don't need to get my partner involved, okay? So keep your voices down." We agreed to his request. The officer took Marcel's wallet, which he had placed on the hood of my car during the search. He took the money out and counted it. There appeared to be around fifty dollars.

"Alright listen, I'm gonna take this little bit of cash and this weed. I'll do a quick search of the car and then you guys will get the fuck out of here," the detective bartered. "Or I can arrest you, and I'll make sure you're on the next bus to The County." Marcel quickly agreed to the deal. The detective pocketed the money and the bags of marijuana. He poked around in my car with his flashlight for a couple of minutes. He finished his search and announced, "There's nothing, let's get out of here."

The younger detective unlocked Nia's cuffs and set her free. The older guy pulled me over to the sidewalk, while everyone else jumped back into my car. He gave me a short speech.

"Let me tell ya something. You don't need to be hanging out with those kinda kids," he informed me. "You can be more than them. Go and find some better friends to ride around with, okay?" I just nodded my head, as he walked away.

The detective's words turned my stomach a little. "Fuck this guy," I said to myself, "What a piece of shit." I got back into my car and we took off. "What was dude saying to you?" Marcel asked me.

"He was just talking more shit," I told him.

As we drove, Nia was getting more and more upset. She was letting it all out, everything that she had bottled up while sitting on that curb. Ant was trying to calm her down. "You've got to relax," he told her. "Come on, you're pregnant. Just breathe."

I assured her that I would have her home soon, but she began to feel very sick. Her pregnant body was full of adrenaline, combined with the heat of the day. I could see in my rearview mirror that she wasn't doing well. I pulled over, so she could get out of the car. Ant sat with her on the curb, as she took deep breaths. Marcel and I wanted to take her to the hospital. She was apprehensive at first, but her situation was not improving. She changed her mind because she began to worry about the baby.

Loretto Hospital was the closest, but it doesn't have a good reputation. I took her to the ER at Oak Park Hospital. Ant jumped out of the car and went to get help. An orderly came out with a wheelchair and rushed her inside. Because she was pregnant, they brought her straight in to see a doctor. Ant went with Nia into the emergency room. Marcel and I went to park the car. We were starting to get nervous. The night was progressively getting more hectic.

Marcel and I were outside smoking and waiting to hear some news. Ant came out of the ER. "They've got her on an IV," he informed us. "They say her blood pressure is way too high. They're trying to stop her from having any major complications." He was clearly a little shook by the situation. We told Ant that we would hang around for a while. There was obviously nothing Marcel and I could do, but we wanted to stay and be supportive.

Nia's mom showed up and she was panicked. We quickly explained to her what happened and then she rushed inside. About thirty minutes later, Ant returned from the emergency room. He let us know that Nia's condition had improved significantly and she was most likely out of the woods. He asked us to wait for him until they moved Nia up to a room. The doctor wanted her to spend the night in the hospital so they could keep an eye on her.

Once Nia was settled in her room, I drove Ant home, but he wasn't ready to go upstairs yet. I felt the same way, because I wasn't ready to go home either. I didn't want to sit around at home, with all of those thoughts and feelings swirling around in my head. I knew it would be better to talk about everything and get it out of our systems.

We decided to hang out on Ant's front steps for a while. We needed to decompress, after the night we were having. We knew that Nia's health was much more important than our stress levels, so we couldn't complain too much. Marcel and I told Ant about what happened with the older detective. He was surprised to hear the story. Ant patted Marcel on the back. "It's way better to get robbed and be free," he told him, "than to be sitting in The County, jo!"

Marcel had turned eighteen earlier that year. That night was his first encounter with the police as an adult. "Man, the stakes are higher for real. I would've been sitting in there for months fighting that case," he said. "That cop is a fucking scumbag, but he did do me a favor, I guess." Marcel knew that he didn't have a chance fighting those charges. He had been living with his older sister in a small apartment because his mom was in prison. They could barely pay the rent and they had no assets, so he would have been stuck in jail.

"But I'm broke now," Marcel continued. "That's all the money I had to my name. Dude didn't need that money. Them detectives get paid, jo. Why did he have to take what little I've got?" I could relate to how conflicted he felt. The police can leave you happy and mad at the same time. I assured him that was the best possible outcome, given the situation. "Just think about being in jail when you lie down," I told him. "Your sister's couch is gonna feel like a king size bed tonight."

Ant wanted to get some sleep. He was going back up to the hospital first thing in the morning. I dropped Marcel off on my way home. After I parked my car, I stood there and looked at it for a minute. I was truly considering slapping a "For Sale" sign in the window.

I went inside and took a shower. The police treated us like dirt and I felt like I had to wash it off. Plus, I had been sweating all day. I tried to lie down, but these encounters with the police were yielding the same result. I felt a restless energy that made sleep seem impossible. It was like a shock to the system, to have reality change so quickly. One minute, you're minding your own business. The next minute, you're at someone else's complete mercy.

I went over the events of that night. I remembered how the detectives never checked our IDs. They weren't interested in who we were or where we were going. They just wanted to search us. It seemed like their goal for the night was to rob people. I guess we looked like good targets.

There was no question that race was a major factor. The detective made it very clear to me that he was racist. His bigoted advice was stuck in my head. It was sad to hear that anyone could view the world that way. Especially someone who had so much power over the people he looked down upon. That conversation made me feel very uneasy. He spoke to me privately, White guy to White guy, my Black friends sitting fifteen feet away. I didn't want to feel associated with that shit. Biting my tongue was the hardest part. I wanted to talk a bunch of shit, but I knew that would've been a bad idea. I chose not to tell everyone what the detective said, because I didn't want to pile on more negativity. That garbage wasn't worth repeating.

While lying there I started thinking about my car again. I knew that Papa Foe had made some valid points about that type of automobile, but I knew it wasn't just the car. I thought about other times that I was stopped by the police in my Eldorado. A couple of months earlier, I was pulled over for gunning it at a stop light.

I was sitting at a red light on Austin Blvd and the guy next to me wanted to race. The light turned green and we both smashed our gas pedals. I jumped ahead and I was feeling good until I saw a cop car sitting in a gas station. The other guy made a quick right turn, which left me as the cops' easiest target.

The police pulled me over. My girlfriend at the time, was the only passenger in the car. The police officers checked my paperwork and they gave me a warning. One of the officers loved the car. He asked questions about the engine size and the horsepower. He even sympathized with me. "I completely understand why you were flooring it," he said. "If I was driving this car, I'd want to race it too, but you can't be speeding like that."

Those cops didn't care to search the car or pat us down. They decided to give some White kids a free pass. They had a legitimate reason to pull me over, but they weren't interested in escalating the situation. They didn't even write me a ticket. I began to imagine the same scenario, but instead with my Black friends riding along. It didn't play out the same way.

The next morning, Nia was released from the hospital. I stopped by her place, later that evening, to see how she was doing. She was feeling much better and her blood pressure was back to normal. She was still angry about the incident with the police. The previous night was her first experience of that nature. "They never gave us a reason why they pulled us over," she said. "They're not allowed to just search us like that! You know that's illegal? My mom thinks we should sue them."

I was only a year older than Nia, but she made me feel like a jaded old man. At nineteen, I was already numb to that type of thinking. I had seen the police throw out their rulebook enough times. I wasn't the least bit surprised by their actions the night before.

I agreed with everything Nia was saying. I knew she just had to vent. That's all anyone can do in that situation. Like most people, Nia's desire to right a wrong by suing the police department faded over time. She went as far as talking to a lawyer, but there was nothing the lawyer could do. We had no evidence. We didn't even know the last names of the detectives.

Over the years, as I came to understand the implications of the events of that night, I have realized the profound impact that they had on me. I was more of an observer in that situation. Ant, Marcel, and Nia were all threatened with jail, while I just stood there with my hands on the car and watched everything transpire. My adrenaline wasn't pumping like it had in previous encounters with the police. I watched a detective take his power and use it solely for personal gain. He even hid his looting from his partner so he could keep it all for himself. I could only imagine how many people he had bullied and robbed in his career. Both detectives had badges, but no identities. They were no different than masked gunmen robbing people in the wilderness. It's disturbing to think that those two guys were ranked police officers.

4

OUTSIDE COOK COUNTY

In December of 1997, I was taking classes at the local community college. I had no exact plan in life, so I figured I might as well get some college credits under my belt. The cost of public college back then was shockingly low compared to nowadays. I was taking mostly business-related classes and getting good grades. On a weekday afternoon, I had an accounting course. When class let out, I decided to do my homework in the library. I had nothing else to do that night, so I was free to chill.

On my way home I stopped to get some gas a couple of blocks from my house. While I was at the pump, Papa Foe pulled into the gas station. He hopped out of his car and he was happy to see me. I hadn't hung out with him for a couple of months, so we caught up. He was heading to his nephew's place, in his old neighborhood. He insisted that I ride with him because he wanted me to meet his nephew. We were around the same age and he thought we would get along. I had nothing on my plate, so I was down to take a ride and kick it.

Papa Foe followed me home so I could park my car. I jumped in with him and we headed out. After a short drive we pulled up to a two-flat, a couple of blocks off of Madison and Pulaski. There was a group of dudes hanging out in front of a building, a few doors down. When they saw Papa Foe get out of the car, they approached us. They greeted him like he was a celebrity. Papa Foe is the kind of guy who, without any words, demands respect. I will admit, at that moment, I felt honored just to be riding with him. The guys on the block treated me like I must be the man too, because I was with Papa Foe. After talking out front for a few minutes, we headed upstairs.

Papa Foe had family living in both flats and the basement apartment. We went up to his sister's place, where his nephew, Marcus, was chilling, watching the Bulls play the Lakers on his antenna TV. Looking back on nights like that, I feel very lucky to have witnessed the greatness of Michael Jordan, playing just down the street at the United Center. That night, as he faced off against Kobe Bryant, it was as if Mike were playing against himself, with a young Kobe proving to the world that he could hang with his idol. None of us could have known how iconic those moments would become, but we knew we were watching sports history. I will always be grateful for that history being a part of my day-to-day life.

After the Bulls ended up killing the Lakers, Marcus pleaded with Papa Foe to give him a ride to his girlfriend's house. She lived in Aurora, which is a forty-five-minute drive at night. It was getting late, so Papa Foe said it was up to me. I wasn't considering objecting to Marcus's request, because I could never deny a man an opportunity to see his woman. We jumped in the car and hit I-290. Around thirty minutes into the trip, the low fuel light came on. We were riding in an early-90s Cadillac Seville. It was a nice car at the time, but it was a gas guzzler. Being a city guy, who rarely drove very far, Papa Foe was becoming nervous about getting stranded in the middle of nowhere. He pulled off at the next exit and we searched for a gas station.

We had no idea where we were. I was especially clueless, because I was sitting in the backseat. We were aimlessly driving through a generic suburban landscape. All I saw were subdivisions and office parks from my window. We finally approached an area that was all lit up. There wasn't a gas station, but there was a convenience store that was open. I jumped out and asked the clerk for directions. When I got back into the car, Papa Foe and Marcus were arguing. Papa Foe was convinced that we were going to run out of gas. "Ayy, the dude told me there's gas about a mile away," I said.

"You better hope we make it man," Papa Foe told Marcus.

We were probably riding on fumes by the time we made it to the pumps. Marcus and I hung outside of the car, while Papa Foe pumped the gas. Which turned out to be an action that we soon regretted. A police car rolled into the gas station. The cruiser pulled right up next to us. A White male officer nodded his head. It was difficult to guess his age range, because he had a serious baby face. The officer appeared to be, not very successfully, trying to grow a mustache. He was definitely not a visually intimidating character. The cop was riding solo and I could clearly see why. There was absolutely nothing going on around there, at 10:30 PM. It seemed as though everyone in the entire area was at home and in bed.

"How you doing officer?" Marcus attempted to be polite.

"I'm doing alright," the cop responded. "Were you guys playing some loud music?"

All of us shook our heads in confusion. "No officer, we weren't playing any music at all," Papa Foe answered.

"Well, I received a noise complaint, not too far from here," the officer informed us. "A vehicle fitting this one's description was driving around and blasting music." His claim sounded like bullshit. He didn't seem confident in what he was saying. I had never heard the police use that accusation before. It seemed very unlikely that anyone had been playing loud music around there.

"That wasn't us." Papa Foe said, "Like I said, we didn't even have any music on." The officer didn't respond. He just stared at us, like he drifted off somewhere. It was a little creepy. "Alright," he said, snapping out of it. "I'm just going to need you guys to hang tight for a couple of minutes." He parked his cruiser in front of Papa Foe's car, in order to block our path.

We leaned on the side of the Seville, while the cop sat in his cruiser. He was visibly talking on his radio.

"Dude is calling for backup." Marcus whispered, "What the fuck jo? Why is he tripping?"

"Chill man!" Papa Foe responded, "He might just be calling my plate in. We all good. My plates are clean." Marcus shook his head, because he wasn't feeling very optimistic about the situation. "We don't even know where we at fam!" Marcus responded. Papa Foe and I couldn't help but to laugh out loud.

"Look at the back of the car man," Papa Foe told Marcus.

NAPERVILLE POLICE was written across the trunk of the cruiser. I knew Naperville was a small city about thirty miles southwest of Chicago, but as far as I could remember, that was the only time I had ever been there in my life. I had never dealt with the police outside of Cook County before then, and I didn't really know what to expect. After a few minutes, the officer emerged from his vehicle, and asked Papa Foe to pull his car away from the pump and into a marked parking spot.

"Why?" Papa Foe replied. "I don't even understand why you're still talking to us. What did we do man?" The officer appeared to be slightly intimidated by Papa Foe.

"Please just do what I asked. There's no need to escalate the situation." The cop's voice cracked a little as he spoke.

"I'm a grown-ass man. I know the law," Papa Foe informed him. "You need to have a reason to hold us for questions." The officer was clearly out of his league, but he was saved by the clock. The backup that he had called for, finally arrived. The cruiser pulled into the gas station and a solo officer stepped out. He was a middle-aged White male, who came across much more confident. He asked to be filled in on the situation. "I told the driver to move his vehicle and he's not complying with my order," the younger cop told him.

"He never told me why," Papa Foe told the older cop. "Look man, we was just getting gas and then we was leaving. We didn't do nothing." The cops stepped away and had a discussion in private. I really couldn't imagine what they were talking about. The younger officer had absolutely no reason to call for backup in the first place. Even if we were playing loud music before he had arrived, that is no reason to call for assistance. There was nothing legitimate that those officers could have been conversing about. I didn't know much about Naperville at the time and I still don't. I do know that it's a primarily White area and it's relatively low in crime.

When they returned, Papa Foe offered them a deal before they could say a word. "We can just get out of here and you guys will never see us again," he said. "I can guarantee that we won't be back in Naperville. I promise that!" His words seemed to irritate the older cop, because he placed his hand by his gun and kept it there.

"We do not need to negotiate with you," the older officer said. "If you don't start following orders, I won't think twice about arresting you." Papa Foe threw his arms up and hung his head. It was clear that we were dealing with a different type of cop than we were accustomed to. The officers came across as slightly robotic. Urban police officers typically will engage in a rational discussion, but these guys weren't interested.

"Now move your vehicle to a parking spot," the older cop demanded. "I'm not interested in anything you have to say until then." Papa Foe reluctantly complied with the officer's orders. The younger cop placed Marcus and I on the front of his car. The older officer led Papa Foe to the trunk of the Cadillac and they began to pat us down. I waited, with my hands on the police cruiser, as the officer searched Marcus first. The adrenaline in my body began to ease up. I had not been feeling afraid. I was mostly feeling confused by the entire situation and the behavior of the younger officer. He appeared to be mentally off and that had made me a little nervous. I was actually kind of happy when the backup officer arrived because we had someone else to deal with.

Papa Foe had done the majority of the talking up until that point. He had general seniority over Marcus and me. I was happy to let him deal with the questions. He had already pissed both cops off and I could tell that he was choosing to bite his tongue by that point. After regaining my focus, I started to get irritated. "What is your reason for searching us?" I said loudly. "You guys still haven't told us what we did wrong." I unintentionally pulled my hands off of the car and turned toward the older cop. The younger officer lunged at me and grabbed me by the wrist. He put me in a wrestling style hold. "Do not take your hands off of the car!" he screamed at me. "Do not make any sudden movements." I placed my hands back on the car and I knew for sure that the younger officer was ready for some action.

"The vehicle matches the one made in a noise complaint," the older officer answered.

"How does a noise complaint lead to a search though?" I asked.

"Well, you guys are acting suspicious," he replied. "Maybe you guys are high on drugs or something."

The officer's remarks pissed me off. He was just throwing around vague accusations, acting as though the combination of his bullshit theories somehow legitimized their actions. It was very obvious that they had targeted us and they just couldn't resist doing an illegal search.

"That's fucking garbage dude!" I blurted out, "You're just throwing shit around now." The younger cop grabbed the back of my head and forced my face onto the trunk. "Who do you think you're talking to?" he said.

"He is an officer of the law. You need to learn some manners," the younger cop declared.

The older officer approached and got into my face. "Put your hands behind your back!" he commanded. I could feel spit hitting my face as he yelled. He handcuffed me with unnecessary force. I felt my right shoulder hyperextend.

After they were finished with their pat down. The older cop collected our IDs to run our names. He looked at our addresses and asked, "What are you guys doing around here anyhow?" It seemed like a question that one of them should have asked us much earlier.

"We're on our way to Aurora," Marcus responded. "My uncle is giving me a ride to my girlfriend's place." The older officer nodded his head, with indifference, and got on the radio in his car.

The younger cop sat me down on a parking curb block, while Papa Foe and Marcus remained with their hands on the cars. The younger officer reached under the dash and popped the trunk of Papa Foe's car. "Is there anything illegal in the vehicle?" he asked. Papa Foe shook his head, "Nah man." I was surprised that he went straight for the trunk, without cause. He completely disregarded proper procedure. I had always heard that the police out in the suburbs went by the book. I guess I had been misinformed.

After finding nothing in the trunk, he moved on to the cabin of the car. He searched around under the driver's seat and popped up with a grin on his face. "So you guys have been smoking some blunts huh?" he asked. He was holding a couple of Black & Mild wrappers.

"That's not a blunt wrapper man," Papa Foe replied. "Those are for smoking, not rolling up weed." The officer looked confused; he didn't seem to understand the difference. I guessed that he had been recently educated on the subject of cigar paper usage. "Nobody rolls weed with those cigarillos. They're too small." Papa Foe explained.

The officer ignored him and placed the wrappers on the hood of the car, as if they were evidence. He continued his search of the vehicle and the older officer returned from his car. He had been running our names and info for at least twenty minutes. By that point in my life, I had learned that the police have different levels of running information. Back then, they didn't have anything comparable to a modern onboard computer. They could radio in a quick search for stuff like outstanding warrants or unpaid fines. Or they could wait to dispatch someone's criminal history. Police officers pick and choose who they want to run a criminal history on. A basic search of three people would not have taken that long. It was clear that those cops were looking for any possible angle they could work with.

"You two have gotten yourselves in a little bit of trouble," the older cops said to Marcus and me.

"But you've got some real priors," he said to Papa Foe. "You must have spent some time in prison, huh?"

"That was a long time ago," Papa Foe looked up and said. "It don't got nothing to do with what's going on right here."

The older cop laughed and said, "Well it's proven that criminals are more likely to commit crimes."

"Isn't the point of serving time in the joint to pay for your crime?" Papa Foe responded. "If I paid my debt, then why the hell are we talking about it?" The older officer wasn't ready to hear something that logical. He stopped laughing and puffed his chest out. He didn't have a reply for Papa Foe's words, so he began to assist the other officer with the vehicle search. Papa Foe won that round. He was able to quickly halt the officer's line of questions and reinforced the fact that we weren't going to be outsmarted by them. I saw how Papa Foe demanded some respect by making short, yet forceful points.

"I'm pretty sure I smell marijuana in the car," the younger cop said. "I think they tried to cover it up when they saw me pull in. Do you smell it?" The older officer leaned into the Cadillac.

"Yeah, I smell something," he said. "I'm going to radio Jack and see where he is." I wondered who 'Jack' was and I was hoping that he was busy. Those cops had been playing games with us for almost an hour. It was getting late and we were nowhere near home.

They were either playing dumb or they really confused the smell of a Black & Mild with the smell of weed. The older officer returned from his car, where he was on the radio. "Jack is on his way," he announced. All of us showed signs of displeasure. It was clear that we weren't going to be leaving anytime soon.

Around ten minutes later, a police SUV pulled into the gas station. The officer hopped out and went to the back of his truck. He reappeared with a big black dog on a leash. I couldn't believe that they actually called for the K-9. Those two cops were not going to leave any stone unturned. Officer Jack explained that the dog was trained to find guns, drugs, and other contraband.

The dog circled the car, sniffing everything in its path. I couldn't really see what the dog was or wasn't doing from where I was sitting. Apparently, the dog made some sort of signal, because they searched the cabin of the car again. After another fruitless inspection. Officer Jack and the K-9 packed up and left. The two officers stepped aside again and talked. "What do you want to do with him?" I heard the younger cop question, as he gestured in my direction. They continued to chat for a couple more minutes and it seemed like they weren't in agreement.

They settled on a decision and approached us. "You guys can go ahead and get out of here," the older cop said. "You need to head that way if you're going to Aurora." He pointed in the direction that he wanted us to travel. It felt more like he was telling us to get out of his jurisdiction than giving us directions. He handed his keys to the younger cop. He stood me up and unlocked my handcuffs. "You got lucky this time, guy," he told me, "You better hope you never see me again." I kept my mouth shut and hopped into the Seville. Papa Foe wasted no time and got the hell out of there.

We returned to the Interstate and headed toward Aurora. Papa Foe let Marcus have it. I couldn't imagine that Marcus was going to ask him for a ride any time soon. I got tired of them arguing, so I decided to refocus the conversation. "What the fuck were those cops on?" I interjected. "They were fishing for any possible reason to arrest us." Papa Foe quickly paused his beef with Marcus in order to share his wisdom.

"That shit wasn't just about arresting us," he informed us. "They had us out there in the cold. Making sure we felt some pain. All I'm wearing is this goddamn hoodie. I ain't even dressed for this shit. They were trying to make us squirm. They was hoping that one of us would start begging. The police get off on that type of shit. I'm happy with both of you though. Neither of you bitched up. We didn't give them no type of satisfaction.

They didn't get to see any of us sweat or nothing."

Once we got to Aurora, Marcus directed us to an apartment building. He hopped out and I jumped into the shotgun seat. Marcus apologized again and went inside. Papa Foe and I headed back to the city. "Ayy, I hear what you were saying, but what was the point of that shit?" I asked Papa Foe. "Those cops didn't accomplish nothing. They just wasted everyone's time."

"First and foremost, they was hoping to arrest one of us or all of us," Papa Foe replied. "When he seen us, he got excited. He thought he had a sure fucking thing. These cops out here don't know nothing. He probably figured we was coming from the city and we must have something illegal in the car. These boys out here watch too much TV and shit. They just operating off of stereotypes. They get a little nervous when they see us, but they hoping to get a little clout back at the station. Arresting some Black motherfuckers from the city is an accomplishment to them. Like a hunter, hanging a goddamn deer head on his wall. We the biggest trophy they can get. Imagine my head up on that motherfucking cop's mantle. Sitting above the fireplace and shit. Them people would be lucky though. They would get to look at my pretty face every fucking day!" Papa Foe started laughing at his twisted scenario and lit up a cigarette.

"But they knew that they didn't have nothing after they searched the car," I said. "Why did they bother calling in the fucking dogs?"

Papa Foe took a long drag off of his cigarette, so I knew he was about to give me another earful of information.

"They was just making sure that we knew the deal. They showed us that they are willing to throw the kitchen sink at some motherfuckers. They hoping we go home and tell everybody to stay out of their jurisdiction, because they ain't playing. Back in the day, the police would straight up tell a Black dude to leave their town and never come back. Nowadays they ain't trying to get sued, so they make you feel it. They saying the same thing without words. Ayy, for real family, that shit works though. I ain't fitting to ride through there again."

On our way back home, Papa Foe told stories about being harassed by the police throughout his life. He couldn't even recount how many times he had been in a situation like the one we had just experienced. When he spoke about real shit, he always got my undivided attention, because he never beat around the bush. He never added drama or emotions to his knowledge. That night he ended up cracking his shell a little. He shared with me some of his deeper feelings.

"That shit wears on you man," he said. "They just keep fucking with people over and over. They just look at you and they assume the worst. And the fucked-up thing is, I was having nothing but righteous thoughts today. I don't think I had one crooked thought all day. Then this dude pulls up and treats us like we must be on some bullshit. Like we must be riding dirty. That motherfucker don't know shit about any of us. He just going off of skin color and stereotypes. They straight up look down on people. Like they above certain people. They just assuming that they don't want us around them. As much as I don't wanna admit it, that shit does fuck with me. To have somebody be against me and he don't even know me. You know what I'm saying? There's nowhere to put them thoughts. There's no way to get any balance in that equation fam. There's only so many times a tiger can get poked before lashing out. I be feeling like I'm fitting to explode sometimes."

After Papa Foe dropped me off, I really started to process everything. I felt like I had a crash course in civil rights. I had gone through the same old bullshit, but with someone who had done it countless times. Papa Foe had all of the answers. He had insight into the psychology of the police. I wasn't stuck questioning why this or that happened. I wasn't tempted to give the police any benefit of the doubt. The fact that the police operated with extreme racial bigotry just burrowed deeper into my brain.

5

WELCOME TO CANADA

I was presented with a unique opportunity in 1999. An extended family member of mine was making an independent movie. The production company had a few crew member jobs that they were looking to fill. I had always been interested in making music and movies. I knew that the experience would be hugely educational. Working on a full-length movie from start to finish would give me usable knowledge far beyond a book or class on the subject. There was one issue, they were making the movie in Detroit. I searched through some apartment listings, just to see if it was financially doable. I found that the rents were extremely cheap compared to what I was accustomed to. The production company wasn't paying very much, but the cost of living was low. I figured that I would regret letting the opportunity slide by, so I decided to go ahead and make it happen.

I ended up working a lot of different jobs and meeting a lot of people on the movie set. We would go out at night as a group, and I quickly got a feel for the area. One of my favorite places to hang out wasn't even in America. Across the Detroit River is Windsor, Canada, a cool little city with a well-known nightlife.

During my time in Detroit, Twan and Devonte came from Chicago to visit. Devonte and I had been cool for years. Everyone called him by the nickname "Tay-O," including most of his family members. He had an uncle and a cousin who lived in Detroit. Twan and Tay-O decided to make the four-hour drive and kick it for the weekend. They showed up on a Friday night. The two of them were pretty tired after their trip, so they just wanted to chill at Tay-O's uncle's house. We hung out and had a few drinks. Tay-O's uncle was full of stories, so we spent the night talking and laughing.

On Saturday night, Twan was itching to go out and hopefully meet some girls. I had spent the day working on the set. I needed to take a shower, so they came over to pick me up. I hopped in the backseat of Twan's car. "So where we going, jo?" Twan asked me. "Where's the action?"

"Let's go to Canada," I responded. Tay-O and Twan laughed.

"Your tripping man," Tay-O said. "Like we fitting to go all the way to Canada."

"Windsor is just on the other side of the river," I told them. "It won't take us no time to get there."

"For real?" Twan said, "That's crazy man. We should do that shit." Tay-O agreed and we headed for the border.

"Either we take the tunnel or the bridge," I said. "The tunnel is a lot quicker."

"What do you mean tunnel?" Twan asked. "You talking about driving under the water?"

"Yeah jo, it only takes a few minutes and then you pop up in downtown Windsor," I replied. Twan wasn't interested in driving through a tunnel that went under a river. The idea made him feel claustrophobic, so we ended up taking the bridge. At that time, U.S. residents only needed a driver's license or state ID to enter Canada. We crossed over the bridge and got in line at the Canadian border checkpoint. When we pulled up to the booth we were greeted by a female officer.

"Welcome to Canada," she said. "Is everyone in the car a citizen of The United States?" We all confirmed our citizenship. She asked a couple of questions and then we showed her our IDs. She walked around the car and did a quick exterior search of the vehicle with her flashlight.

"One moment," she said, "I'll be right back." She went inside her booth and picked up the phone.

She closed her window, so we weren't able to hear what she was discussing. I was surprised by the delay. I had traveled through those checkpoints many times before and never had any issues. Every previous time, they waived the car right through after they saw valid American IDs. I could tell by the expression on her face that something was up. She opened her window and directed us to pull over to another search area, where we were met by two male officers. They asked us to get out of the car so they could do a full vehicle search.

We stood there waiting while they inspected every inch of Twan's car. The Canadian Border Services officers were more thorough than a typical police search. They looked for hidden compartments and pulled on plastic pieces to see if they were loose. One of the officers laid on a mechanic's creeper and slid under the car. He searched the entire undercarriage. After finding nothing anywhere in or under the car, they called for the K-9s. Twan started to get very irritated by all of this.

"What's up?" he questioned them. "You guys looked everywhere and didn't find nothing. Why do you need to bring the dogs in now?"

"Sir, this is standard procedure," one of the border officers replied. "Please be patient." I laughed to myself, because Americans are not known for having much patience.

Another officer appeared with two German Shepherds and they began to circle the car. One of the dogs became focused on the floor behind the driver's seat. This prompted the officers to examine the area again. By the time the dogs had finished sniffing around, I realized that we had been stuck at the border for over an hour. I assumed that they had to be satisfied with their inspection and they were going to finally let us through. My hopes were met by additional demands. They asked us to enter the office area for individual searches.

The border officers didn't find anything of interest when conducting the personal searches of us. Instead of letting us go on with our night, they asked us to take a seat. A different officer came to gather our IDs and asked us to wait while they ran our information. At that point, I felt like they were determined to keep us out of their country.

We sat there and waited for over thirty minutes. Then the officer who was running our IDs reappeared with some backup. He gave Twan and I our licenses back and held on to Tay-O's. "Sir, after running your information," he told Tay-O, "we have discovered that you have a felony on your criminal record. We have made the decision to deny all of you entry into Canada, at this time."

"Anything you found is old," Tay-O replied. "I've dealt with those charges."

"I understand, but we have made our decision," the officer said. "If you wish to visit Canada in the future, you may file an application and your status will be redetermined." He handed Tay-O his ID and escorted us back to Twan's car. We were guided to an area where we could turn around and head back over the bridge.

"What the fuck man?" Twan said to me. "You didn't say nothing about having to get searched."

"I swear jo, I've been through there a bunch of times," I answered. "They've never done any of that shit before. It usually takes a few minutes and they just let you through." I felt bad, because it was my idea to hang out in Windsor. I never expected to waste two hours at the border just to be sent back to America.

"You ever went through there with some Black people?" Tay-O asked me. I thought about his question and realized what had just happened. "Naw man," I said. "Fuck! I've only gone over there alone or with White people. I didn't even think about that shit. My bad, this whole thing is on me."

"Don't trip jo, it's all good," Tay-O replied. "We just learned some shit tonight. The Canadian border be looking at Blacks the same way the cops in America do. They probably wasn't ever planning on letting us in."

We had lost our momentum for the night. Those wasted hours sapped our desire to go out. We decided to head back to Tay-O's uncle's place and lay low. When we arrived, Tay-O's uncle was happy to see us. He was an old guy who enjoyed having an audience. We told him what happened and he wasn't surprised. "Man, that's how it is!" Tay-O's uncle said. "They don't just be letting us Black folks through there. That's why I don't even bother trying to go over to Windsor. They don't want us in their country."

On Sunday afternoon, Twan and Tay-O stopped by my place before heading back to Chicago. "I'm going the speed limit all the way back home," Twan declared. "I'm not even trying to talk to anyone wearing a uniform." Tay-O was trying to convince Twan to wait until dark before hitting the road. Tay-O preferred the anonymity provided by the night when traveling on the interstate. Twan eventually agreed with Tay-O's position. They delayed their trip because of the color of their skin.

The whole thing was just sad to me. All of the times that I had crossed that border and they never gave me any trouble. Their approach completely changed when they saw some Black faces. This was definitely not a matter of coincidence or randomness. Then to find out that local Black people rarely attempt to visit Canada. It made me think about how many things I took for granted as a White person.

Years later, when the term "White privilege" became part of American vernacular, I often thought of that night. I'd heard many White people dispute or take offense to the term. They felt like it was an overblown concept, or a form of whining used by non-Whites. I was well aware of my own "White privilege" long before the term was popularized. As a White guy, I was viewed as a friend and welcomed through border checkpoints. That was a privilege. Black people were not accorded that type of

49

treatment. I can say with absolute certainty that "White privilege" is real and that the subject does not need to be debated.

6

100-MILE BORDER ZONE

Around a year later, Tay-O and I took a trip to California for no specific reason other than to chill in SoCal for a week. We knew we would be able to stay with members of Tay-O's family throughout Southern California. His extended family was huge, with aunts, uncles, and cousins all over the country, and, somehow, he knew most of them.

At that time in my life, I had just started to learn about music production and audio engineering. One of Tay-O's cousins in LA had connections to a recording studio. His cousin told us that he would take us up there and show us around. That information sealed the deal for me, so we booked some plane tickets. We flew into LAX and rented a car at the airport. We took a short drive to Tay-O's aunt's place, near Inglewood in South Central.

Over the next few days, we were in constant motion. We went up to Hollywood and The Valley, over to Santa Monica and down to Long Beach, visiting people and places. We were having a good time and getting the most out of our car. Tay-O rented the car in his name, so he did all the driving. I was happy to relax and soak up the environment. Tay-O's cousin took us to the studio, which was in Burbank. The engineer told us about all of the equipment and showed us how the space was designed. We were able to observe some vocal recording and audio mixing. Tay-O and I had limited knowledge about those things, so that experience was very informative for us.

The next day, we headed down to San Diego to see a couple of Tay-O's cousins. We just hung around the beach and relaxed in the sun. After staying a couple of nights, we headed back up to LA. We had to catch our flight back to Chicago the next day. We took Interstate 5 north to Los Angeles. About forty-five minutes into our trip, we were forced to go through a checkpoint near San Clemente. We were still well within the territory of the United States, so we couldn't understand why we had to go through a border checkpoint. Later on, I learned about the "100-mile border zone," and that Tay-O and I were stopped at what is called an interior checkpoint.

The "100-mile border zone" is a federal regulation that allows U.S. Border Patrol agents to search vehicles and people within one hundred miles of any international border. Although the Fourth Amendment protects American citizens against arbitrary stops and searches, this federal regulation is still allowed to continue. It seemed crazy to me that there were agents whose entire job was to profile people.

We waited in a long line of vehicles for half an hour. When we finally arrived at the booth, we were greeted by an agent, a White guy. He was wearing mirrored aviator sunglasses and had a big mustache, looking like a character in a bad cop movie. This made me a little nervous.

"Where are you traveling from and what is your destination?" he asked us.

"We came from San Diego and we're going to LA," Tay-O told him.

"Do you have any illegal drugs or firearms in the vehicle?" the agent asked.

"No," we both replied. He slowly walked around the car, doing a visual inspection. When he returned to the booth, he asked to see our IDs.

"You're both from Illinois, huh?" he asked us. "What brings you to California?"

Tay-O explained that we were just visiting for the week. He stared at our IDs and looked at our faces. This continued for about twenty seconds. He was definitely considering how he wanted to proceed with us.

"So, this car is a rental?" he asked.

"Yes, sir," Tay-O responded. "We rented it at LAX. That's where we're flying out of."

The agent closed his window and picked up his walkie talkie. Tay-O and I knew that this was a bad sign. When he was finished with his back-and-forth, he directed us to pull into the secondary search area.

We parked in the designated space and waited for further instructions. We couldn't understand what was going on. How could two Americans, with valid identifications, be searched at a checkpoint? The Border Patrol Stations were supposed to be focused on immigration, but we were clearly citizens of The United States. I later learned that speech was something that border agents focused on closely. Tay-O and I both spoke in a way that was clearly American. The agent could not possibly have questioned our citizenship. He never offered us a reason on why we needed to be searched.

After waiting for at least thirty minutes, an agent approached our vehicle. He had us step out of the car so he could do a full inspection. That part was very similar to our experience at the Canadian Border, with the agent's fruitless search ending in the same result. He called for the K-9s to come and give our car the sniff test. Another agent arrived with two dogs and led them around the car. One of the dogs hopped up on the back bumper and looked in the trunk. Our suitcases were the only things in the trunk and the agent had already gone through them.

The agent insisted that the dog was signaling something. I personally felt like the dog was just being a dog. I was very suspicious of the process at that point. Dogs sniff things, jump on stuff, and make noises all the time. Nothing that the trained K-9 was doing was out of the ordinary, for any dog. The agent began tugging on the carpet and the plastic pieces in the trunk. I thought he was going to break something, because he was being very aggressive.

"What do you have back here?" he asked us. "Do you have some drugs hidden somewhere?" We assured him that there was nothing illegal in the trunk. "You better come clean now," the agent informed us, "because I'll tear this carpet right out and see what's underneath."

"Please don't tear the carpet out man," Tay-O responded. "The rental company might charge me for that." The agent continued to poke around and began to knock on different sections of the trunk and rear bumper. "The K-9 knows what it's doing," he told us, "he wouldn't have signaled here for no reason."

"Just wait here and I'll be back," the agent continued. Around ten minutes later, the agent returned with his superior. They both inspected the entire car again. "Are you two running drugs from the border?" the superior agent asked. "What's your story again?" Just as Tay-O began to speak, the superior agent cut him off.

"Hold on!" he demanded, "Don't say a word." He grabbed Tay-O by the arm and escorted him to the opposite side of the car. He began to question Tay-O quietly, so that I couldn't hear his responses. After he was finished, he came over and began to question me. He was clearly attempting to see if our stories matched up. We had nothing to hide, so the agent's tactic didn't produce any results.

The superior agent gathered our IDs and went inside the building. We sat and waited with the other agent, in awkward silence. Eventually, the superior agent returned and he gave us our IDs back. "Nothing on them," he told the other agent, "but go ahead and get your tools out." They began dismantling different pieces of the trunk. They became visibly frustrated because they were not finding anything stashed away. After taking apart most of the trunk and the rear-end of the car, they decided to take a break. It was hot outside and they were both sweating. The agents went inside to cool off in the air conditioning, leaving the rent-a-car in pieces, while Tay-O and I sat on a curb and cooked in the desert heat.

The agents returned after their break. "It's your lucky day, because we've decided to let you two continue on your way," the superior agent said, "but just so you both know, we could have lifted the car up and done a more thorough inspection. I'm talking about taking the wheels and tires off. Removing the muffler. Disassembling the door panels. So yeah." He was clearly looking for us to show him some gratitude.

"Thank you sir," I said, "We really appreciate it." The words that came out of my mouth made my chest tighten up. After sitting through an absolutely targeted search, I was the one thanking him. It felt un-American to essentially be kicked around and then to thank the aggressor for stopping. The national government arbitrarily searching the people is not something we believe in. That day, Tay-O and I experienced something that would be expected from a fascist system. Government agents in a land where "all men are created equal" should not be engaging with citizens in that manner. My view of individual rights in America had, once again, been dramatically altered.

The agents reassembled the pieces that they had removed. They were able to get everything pretty much back in place. We looked the car over and found that they had done some damage, but it wasn't very noticeable. We were relieved to be done with the stress, but we were equally relieved to get out the heat. Tay-O put the air conditioner on full blast and we headed for Los Angeles.

"What is the deal man?" I asked Tay-O. "We've got no type of luck at checkpoints!"

"Them border agents are on the same bullshit as the police," Tay-O answered.

"They had us sitting there for over an hour," I said. "They didn't even have a reason to search us."

"That whole thing was racial jo," Tay-O replied. "When the guy in the booth saw my Black ass pull up, he was immediately thinking about searching us." I thought about what Tay-O was saying.

"But I'm not Black, so you would think that would balance out some of that profiling shit," I said.

"When you are with Black people, the police see you as Black," Tay-O answered. "They looking at the situation like, if you're with Blacks then you might as well be Black." Those words have stuck with me very deeply; Tay-O said them in such a matter-of-fact way. There was no question in his mind that law enforcement was fixated on targeting Black people.

We flew back to Chicago the next day. We had a good trip to Southern California, but not without some drama. It was the type of drama that I've never experienced when alone or with other White people. I have done my fair share of traveling since then. I've passed through many border checkpoints and customs throughout the world. I lived in Los Angeles for a few years and traveled to San Diego several times. I passed through the same checkpoint, either by myself or with my girlfriend at the time. Every time the border agents just let me go right through without more than a couple of questions.

After two negative interactions with border agents, I felt like my eyes opened even wider. It was clear to me that there were officers, from local departments up to the federal level, utilizing racial targeting. That was when I realized how much racial prejudice was an all day, everyday issue. As a White person, I still didn't understand how much being Black means being treated as an outsider, especially in a negative way; how too often, White people will see the race before the person. What I've come to realize is that the profiling doesn't necessarily stop with cops and federal agents; Black people spend their entire lives being profiled by their fellow Americans, and too often are denied the privilege of being treated as individuals.

7

OUT FRONT WITH THE
YOUNGINS

In 2002, I moved into my parent's three-flat apartment building in Forest Park. Over the previous two years, I had learned a lot about music production and audio engineering. I befriended some older dudes that were on the frontline of the digital revolution. They taught me about computers, programs, and equipment. The music industry was in a major transition. The recording of instruments and vocals with analog audio tape was dying. Computers had recently become capable of processing and storing audio tracks without a loss of quality. They gave the average person the ability to record music at a fraction of the price. A couple thousand dollars could buy everything needed to record music digitally, while analog studios required an investment of tens of thousands of dollars.

I felt like I had gathered enough information to construct my own recording and production space. My parents allowed me to build a soundproof studio in the basement of the building, and I had saved up enough money to get things going. Tay-O also decided to put some of his money in. That enabled me to have everything up and running in a matter of months. It was nothing fancy, but we had what we needed to get the job done.

A few months later, a friend from high school referred me to an eighteen-year-old kid he had met. The kid was making beats on some old school equipment and had notebooks full of rhymes. I gave him a call and set up a time for him to come over. A couple of days later I met Giovanni, who went by "Gio" for short. He played me a couple of beats that he had made and rapped some of his rhymes. I liked the direction he was headed in. We were both influenced by many of the same rappers and producers. He came across as extremely driven and focused on his goals. I could sense that he was ready to put in some work.

At that point, everyone that I had worked with was my age or older, artists that had some experience under their belts. I was fortunate enough to be gifted a massive amount of knowledge, so I felt like I should pay it forward. I decided to collaborate with Gio and show him the ropes. We scheduled a time to get to work on a song.

A couple of days later, Gio returned to the studio. He brought his friend Lorenzo, who went by the nickname "Zoeski." Gio informed me that they wanted to be a rap duo. I soon learned that Zoeski had just turned sixteen years old, so I was a little skeptical of the idea. I had already heard some of Gio's stuff, so I decided to throw the young kid straight into the fire. "Have you ever rapped on a microphone before?" I asked him.

"Naw jo, I ain't never been in a studio before," Zoeski responded.

"Go put the headphones on and let's see what's up," I told him.

He did a mic check and grinned when he heard his own voice coming through the headphones. I played an instrumental and told him that I was recording. He looked nervous, as he was feeling out the tempo. He started rapping and he was all over the place. He looked a little discouraged, but I motioned for him to continue. He kept going and he started to settle into the beat. His raps were sloppy at times, but that can improve with practice.

He had a great recording voice, which isn't something that can be learned.

I felt like Gio and Zoeski could make a solid duo, because they brought different things to the table. Gio had his eye on the prize and I knew that he was full of ideas. Zoeski's personality was twice as big as his frame and he appeared to have an endless supply of energy. I knew that they were going to be a long-term project, but I felt like they could progress quickly with some help. They started coming over a few days a week and they showed some improvement every time.

In a short amount of time, they became like little brothers to me. They always showed up with enthusiasm and reckless optimism. At twenty-four years old, I was already exhausted by the real world. I liked having them around. They always filled the space with energy. Over time, they got better and better. I started to think they had the potential to make some hit songs, and I began to focus more of my time toward their development.

On a Sunday afternoon, in the spring of 2003, I was sitting with Gio and Zoeski on the front stairs of my building. They had just come from the park where they were playing basketball, both still sweating and trying to catch their breath. Hooping is like a religion on the West and South Sides of Chicago, and a pick-up game in a park is an intense battle of highly skilled athletes; our neighborhood alone had produced many collegiate and NBA players. Just like so many other Chicago kids, Gio and Zoeski felt like they could compete at a high level.

They were discussing their recent accomplishments on the court and joking about some of their failures. Zoeski stood up to reenact a fadeaway jump shot he had made. At that moment, I saw a police car coming down my block. I didn't think anything of it. I brought my attention back to Zoeski's animated account of his basketball heroics.

The cop car pulled up to the curb, right in front of us. There was only one officer in the car. That was unusual, but I guess they were hoping for a lazy Sunday. The officer was a stocky White guy. I couldn't imagine that he would've been able to catch anyone in a foot race. He stepped out of the car.

"What gang are you guys in?" he asked us.

"What?" Zoeski responded. "Why you coming at us like that, jo?" Zoeski's youthful boldness with the police officer caught me off guard. "Ayy, ayy, slow down," I told Zoeski. I wasn't looking to make a spectacle in front of my crib.

"What did you say to me?" the officer asked. "You think you're fucking tough?" The cop charged across the sidewalk straight for Zoeski.

I jumped up and got in between them. "Back up man!" I told the officer. "This is private property. You can't just step across the sidewalk like that." I wasn't planning on using that tone with him, but his aggression really irritated me. He immediately realized that I was correct and he stepped back onto the sidewalk. Our chests had bumped a little when I jumped up and he took offense to that. "You fucking touch me again and you're going to jail!" he told me. He turned almost purple with anger as he held his finger in my face.

"You think you're a badass?" the cop continued. "Come on! Let's find out." His attempt to bait me into a fight almost succeeded. I felt my arm cocking back, like my soul was telling me to throw a punch. My brain took over and I stepped back.

"For what? We didn't do nothing," I responded. "You're the only person here that's getting crazy. Why don't you just get in your car and go? We can walk away like this never happened." He got back into his car and I thought he was actually taking my advice. Instead, he grabbed his radio mic and called for backup. Hearing him say my address into the microphone made me more irritated. I felt like he was making a scene in front of my parent's building over nothing.

He got back out of his car. "All you guys should get off the stairs and come stand on the sidewalk," he said.

"We wasn't doing nothing though," Zoeski replied. "Why are you tripping so hard?"

"I saw you throwing up a gang sign," the officer responded.

"I was just doing a basketball motion," Zoeski answered. "I wasn't throwing nothing up. And for real though, Black people don't really be throwing up no gang signs no more. This ain't the eighties man."

His backup arrived; a couple of uniformed officers approached.

"Look man, you know this shit is racial," I said. "You're getting all aggressive because he's Black."

"That's got nothing to do with it," the officer quickly replied. "I'm not racist or nothing." He looked over at the two cops who just showed up. He appeared to be embarrassed by the situation. "What the hell is going on here?" the lead officer asked him.

"I saw this guy throwing up a gang sign," he responded, "and now they're refusing to come off the stairs."

"You keep saying gang sign. What gang?" I asked him. "What did you think he threw up?" The officer froze a little and I could see his mind churning.

"I'm not one hundred percent sure," he said. "I was halfway down the block."

"You don't even know what you think you saw?" I asked him.

"It looked like Latin Kings to me," the officer replied.

Zoeski jumped in: "Do I look like a Latin King to you man? There ain't even no Kings around here."

"You could be," the cop answered. "They've got some Black members. There's some Latin Kings down on 16th Street."

"Come on jo," Zoeski declared, "you're tripping!"

"This whole thing is racial man," I said. "You know what you were doing. You was just making assumptions."

"I'm tired of your mouth," the officer shouted at me. "You're about to get cuffed!"

"He's not racist," the lead officer chimed in. "He's a good guy and you need to shut up right now."

Right then, my dad came out of the gangway (a common term in Chicago for the walkway between buildings). "What the hell is going on?" he yelled. "I own this building."

"Oh, hi sir," the stocky officer replied. "I was just questioning these guys because I saw him throwing up a gang sign."

"Oh yeah, what gang?" my dad asked.

"I believe it was Latin Kings," the officers answered.

"Who this guy?" my dad pointed to Zoeski. "He doesn't look like a Latin King to me."

Zoeski busted out with laughter. The stocky cop looked even more embarrassed. Then the lead backup officer took command of the situation.

"Sorry for the commotion sir," the lead officer said to my dad. "We're going to step to the side and discuss this. Just give us a minute."

The officers huddled up on the street and spoke quietly. The cop that we had been arguing with looked pissed and he got into his car. The lead officer came back to the sidewalk. "Okay look, we're going to let you guys slide on this one," he said. "We're about to get out of here and everyone is going to move on with their day. Alright?" He pointed his finger at me and puffed up. "You need to watch yourself!" he informed me. "Trust me, I'm not going to forget your face." We nodded our heads in agreement and they took off.

I didn't feel like being outside anymore. After every unwarranted altercation with the police, I felt like I just wanted to stay inside. Simply walking a block down to the corner store felt risky. I wondered if the police knew how paranoid they made people with their behavior. Maybe they didn't care. At that point, I started to feel like the police didn't understand the duties of their occupation. They are paid to serve and protect. That cop wasn't serving or protecting anything. He was harassing us for his own personal reasons.

We headed down to the basement and I started up my computer. "Man jo, you was really getting loud with that cop," Gio said to me. "I thought they was taking you to jail for sure."

"Somebody had to say something and you wasn't saying shit!" I replied. We all laughed.

"I couldn't get a fucking word in," Gio said. "You two wouldn't stop running your mouths."

"You was coming at that cop like a lawyer, jo," Zoeski said to me. "You had him stumbling over his words. He was standing there looking stupid. That shit was crazy."

"The police have had me hemmed-up on some bullshit, too many times," I responded. "I just didn't feel like playing with them today."

After chilling out a little, we got to work on some music.

The most telling thing about that day was the cops' reaction when my dad came out front. They saw a sixty-year-old White man and they completely changed their demeanor. All of a sudden, they were apologetic and they were calling him 'sir.'

Later on, I thought about how bold I had gotten with that cop. At the time, I was just reacting to the situation. I wasn't deliberately being forceful. I realized that a couple of factors really fueled my behavior. First of all, the fact that we had been on private property gave me some power. It wasn't much in actuality, but more than I had when being pulled out of a car or getting searched in a park. Two, I had so much anger built up inside of me. I was so tired of the racial targeting. I had sat on many porches with many White people in my life. We never had to deal with that type of aggression.

That cop was on bullshit and I had to call him out. I didn't really care if I went to jail. The hostility I felt toward the police had been pent-up for too long. I knew that I was lucky not to have been arrested that day. I was sure I would see those cops again and I hoped that they weren't seeking some type of revenge.

8

HARLEM AVENUE HARASSMENT

Over the next year, I began to accumulate more and more studio work. I continued to spend some of my free time working with Gio and Zoeski, providing them songs with high-quality mixes and production. I took some pictures of them and designed a CD cover. Between them they didn't have enough money for my time, so I decided to write up a contract. We agreed to a fair split of any future income. With Zoeski being a minor, I needed his mom to sign the contract for him.

Armed with CDs, they went everywhere promoting our music. Gio was actively pursuing every opportunity he could find. He got the attention of a promoter who booked some shows for them. Gio found singers to collaborate with—at the time, radio stations preferred rap songs that featured a singer on the chorus. One of the singers Gio brought to the studio was named Deshawna, she went by "DeDe." We had worked with several singers, but she was the best fit for our style.

On a weekday afternoon, in the summer of 2003. Zoeski, Gio, and I hopped into my car. We had scheduled a recording session with DeDe.

We were working on a new song that was perfect for her voice. DeDe normally would take the L train to my place. She lived only four stops away, but I wanted to get to work as soon as possible. Going to pick her up was quicker than the train. Right when we were getting back to the studio, we ran into some trouble.

As I was turning onto my block, I noticed a police car pull out of the alley. The marked car made the turn with us. Halfway down the block, they flashed their lights. We were only a few buildings away from my home. None of us could figure why they pulled us over. I used my turn signal and I wasn't speeding. They just sat behind us and I began to get restless. I assumed they were waiting for backup. Based on previous experience, I knew that things were about to get more intense than a routine traffic stop.

I hoped that when the police saw my address, they would be cool, because I was pulled over on my own block. A few minutes later, an unmarked detective car pulled over to the curb in front of us. A couple of detectives got out and stood watch while the uniformed cops approached. I looked in my rearview mirror and my stomach sank. The stocky officer we had argued with the year before was walking up to my window.

He lowered his head and asked for my license and registration. He looked at everyone in the car individually. He didn't say a word. He just looked at each of us for several seconds, making it clear that he remembered our faces. His lack of words unnerved me a bit. I would have preferred that he talked a little shit. His blank stare showed us that he was dead serious. He went back to his car to run my information. His partner hung on the curb and chatted with the detectives.

I had only seen that cop twice since our altercation the previous year. The first time, I was behind him in line at the store, but I made sure that he didn't see me. The second time, I was getting gas and he pulled into the station. He just sat there mean mugging me and then he pulled off. After that, I figured that he was going to eventually stop and search me. The odds were stacked against me. It was just a matter of time before he would get a good opportunity for harassment. I couldn't believe that he got all three of us in one car. He definitely had a clean shot at some revenge. I just hoped that he wasn't going to take it too far.

The stocky officer returned to my window and handed me my paperwork. "Everything's good there," he said, "but I'm going to need all of you to step out of the vehicle, two at a time."

"What did we do?" I asked.

"Shut up and get out of the car," he responded. He put his hand on his gun and I decided to take his advice. Zoeski and I were removed and placed on the hood of my car. The uniformed officers then removed DeDe and Gio from the backseat and placed them on the trunk. They began to pat them down. I assumed that the detectives were going to search Zoeski and me, but they just stood there leaning on their car.

"Ayy man, we didn't do nothing," Gio said. "Why you searching me?"

"I saw you sniffing dope," the stocky cop answered.

"What are you talking about dude?" Gio replied. "Because I know you didn't see that."

"I saw you through the window," the officer told him. "You were right there in the backseat sniffing something." Gio started laughing.

"I ain't no dopehead man," he informed the officer. "You ain't fitting to find nothing on me."

"We were a block away from my building," I chimed in. "Why would anyone do that? Like who couldn't wait a couple of minutes? That doesn't make any sense."

"How would I know where you guys were going?" the stocky cop replied.

"Once you saw my address, you should've realized your theory wasn't adding up," I responded. The lead detective popped up and pointed his finger at me. "Watch your mouth," he snapped. "You're fucking pushing it."

When we got pulled over. I told myself that I was going to be chill, but after I heard the cop's reason for stopping us, my intended approach went out the window. Maybe Zoeski and Gio's youthfulness had rubbed off on me more than I realized. I knew one thing for sure, getting harassed on my own block again really pissed me off.

The uniformed officers finished their searches of DeDe and Gio. They began to pat Zoeski and me down. The stocky cop searched my pockets. "You know you're just being petty," I told him. "Your reason for stopping us is garbage."

"Well, you also didn't signal when you turned off of Jackson," he responded.

I turned a little to look at him and he stepped back into a defensive stance. "That's bullshit man!" I said. "Now you're just adding on some shit."

Zoeski jumped in, "I know he signaled for sure!"

The lead detective stepped up and grabbed me by the neck. He drove me into the hood of my car, squeezing my jugular. "Shut the fuck up!" he ordered me. "If you say another word you're going to jail!" He pulled me over to the hood of his car.

"You search the car," he told the uniformed cops. "I'll finish searching this fucking guy."

"If you're not answering a question," the detective told me, "then you're not speaking."

He continued to hold me by the neck as he went through my pockets. The uniformed officers found nothing illegal as they searched through my car and trunk. The detectives both gave the stocky officer a look of displeasure, like he had promised them something good and didn't deliver.

"Everyone go ahead and get back in the car," the lead detective said, as he took command of the situation. "Just hang tight a minute while we figure this out."

We waited as the officers talked. When they finished their discussion, the lead detective began to hover near my door. I wasn't sure what he was doing. It felt like he was planning on pulling me back out of the vehicle. A few minutes later, the stocky officer came to my window.

"I went ahead and wrote you a ticket for failure to signal," he told me. "All the court information and instructions are on the back." I took the ticket and kept my mouth shut. After the uniformed cops got back into their car, the lead detective popped his head through my window.

"Listen to me closely, okay," he told me. "I'm out here five days a week and I've got my eyes on you. If I ever see you take that kinda attitude with an officer again, you're going to jail, guy. I will personally put the cuffs on you and drag your ass to lockup. Got it?"

The detective's short speech was the last thing I wanted to hear. Knowing that there were multiple police officers in my neighborhood that were out to get me was unnerving. I figured that I might as well attempt some damage control.

"Look, I wasn't trying to be disrespectful or cocky or something," I tried to explain, "it's just that we've got a history with that guy. He came at us last year over nothing. He's just looking for any reason to mess with us." The detective's demeanor changed a little.

"Oh yeah, so you think he's got a personal issue with you guys?" he asked.

"Yeah, one hundred percent," I responded.

"Alright, I hear what you're saying," he said. "But you need to watch your mouth. I'm not going to tolerate that shit in the future." I nodded my head and he walked back to his car.

I was happy to have lessened some of the tension. The detective seemed to be somewhat understanding and less eager to arrest me in the future. I felt like I dodged a bullet, until I looked at the ticket on my lap. It ended up costing me seventy-five dollars and a knock on my driving record. That stocky cop was able to manufacture a little bit of revenge. I saw him a few months later at Dunkin' Donuts and he acted like he didn't know me. I assumed that he considered us even and that he had moved past our little beef.

After shaking off some of the anxiety, we got to work. DeDe sang the best vocals that she had ever recorded. The adrenaline fueled her. She channeled her hostility toward the police and turned it into something good. I could sense that she was very proud of her performance.

"Next time I come over, I'm taking the train," she joked. "It's too risky riding with you dudes!"

"Yeah, but them police got you turned up," Zoeski replied. "You came in here and lit the mic up."

"But for real though, those police was on some bullshit!" Dede responded. "I hope that chubby cop gets fired. He's out here just making shit up."

We wrapped everything up and called it a night. We gave DeDe a ride home, without any unexpected stops. I was happy to get home and relax. It was a relief not to be riding around on the streets, looking at every vehicle moving and hoping that none of them were cop cars. That day, I had experienced another fabricated stop and search at the hands of police. With three of the four people in my car being Black, I really wasn't surprised.

That was around the time when the internet was becoming a reliable source of information. I decided to get serious about researching laws and individual rights. I knew that the police had the power to suppress those liberties whenever they chose to go rogue, but information is still a little power—the incidents that I had been through with Gio and Zoeski had really shown me that. I realized that on both occasions, I had made some valid points that had the effect of changing the cops' approach. I had Papa Foe to thank for some of that strategy.

Knowledge is useless on a police officer who is hell-bent on making an arrest, but it's always best to have the information. The police are less likely to bully someone who they know is informed.

Throughout the next year, Gio and Zoeski made some big strides with their music dreams. Gio found a manager who knew some people in the industry. I worked with the manager to get our music out to the radio stations and record labels. We were able to gain some interest from a few labels. We began negotiations with a major company when suddenly the wheels fell off.

Zoeski had gotten himself arrested on some serious charges. He was in the wrong place at the wrong time. Not to say he wasn't at fault, but it was a situation he should have walked away from. He had recently turned eighteen and was therefore tried as an adult. Zoeski ended up getting sentenced to five years in the penitentiary. Gio kept trying to push forward, but no one was interested in doing business with a rap duo that had one member in prison.

9

OPEN MIC FIGHT NIGHT

After Zoeski was sent off to the penitentiary, I began focusing more of my studio time on other rappers. Gio had lost some of his desire to write and produce. It seemed as though he wanted to wait out Zoeski's prison sentence and pick up where they left off. I continued to hang out with him, but we rarely worked on music. Throughout the time I was developing Gio and Zoeski, I was also working with many other artists.

Marcel and I had made several songs together. Back when we were teenagers, Marcel was one of the best freestyle rappers around. He was always ready and willing to get into a rap battle. I had never seen anyone get the best of him. Like a lot of gifted freestyle rhymers, Marcel struggled with writing a complete song. He was able to rap for ten straight minutes, but he grappled with writing a catchy chorus.

Marcel's ego could barely fit inside my little studio. He typically disregarded any suggestions or advice. It wasn't uncommon for us to get into arguments while working on a song, but time wore down some of Marcel's arrogance. After watching a couple of kids like Gio and Zoeski get more recognition than him, he realized that he needed to change his approach. He started to listen to my advice and focused more of his energy on writing memorable choruses and became much more receptive to hearing constructive criticism and making some adjustments.

On a Saturday night, Marcel and I were working on a song. His friend, Trav, who grew up on his block, was hanging out while we worked. I had become pretty cool with Trav and I didn't mind him chilling at our recording sessions—he was a very intimidating dude and Marcel usually took his input without much pushback. We were able to get some solid work done and wrapped everything up around midnight. Marcel wanted to hit a little club that was doing a hip hop night. They would host rap battles on the stage and Marcel wanted to get up there and put his name on the list.

The club was in Wicker Park, which was only a fifteen-minute drive from my place. Wicker Park had once been considered a rough neighborhood, but it was taken over by hipsters and yuppies a few years prior. Nights when clubs featured hip hop music produced a unique blend of cultures in the neighborhood. We arrived and saw that there was a pretty lengthy line out front. We hoped that we could squeeze in before they hit maximum occupancy.

After getting through the door and paying admission, Marcel went to throw his name into the ring. The place was packed and buzzing with bass. Trav and I went to the bar to grab some drinks. We searched out Marcel and found him with the dude who was in charge of the battle. He was attempting to talk his way onto the list.

"Come on jo!" Marcel said. "You know me fam. You know I'm gonna murder these cats. You gotta put me up there."

The promoter was looking at his list and shaking his head. "I'm already filled up bro," he said. "You should've got here earlier."

Marcel wasn't taking 'no' for an answer. His confidence overwhelmed the guy. The promoter eventually caved in and added Marcel to the list. We carved out a spot and chilled for a while. A pretty girl caught Marcel's eye and he struck up a conversation with her. We weren't the least bit surprised by that. I personally would have been mentally preparing for the heated battle on stage, but Marcel wasn't sweating it. He was born ready to freestyle.

After a few minutes, a giant White dude approached Marcel and the girl. He appeared to be angry about something. The guy was the size of an offensive lineman, but he didn't intimidate Marcel in the slightest. Marcel was tall and skinny as a teenager, but he had been lifting weights for years. Most people would have thought twice before picking a fight with him at that point in time. It turned out that the big White dude was the girl's ex-boyfriend. He grabbed her by the arm and started to pull her away.

"Come on, let me talk to you for a minute," he said to her.

"Get your fucking hands off of me!" she shouted.

Marcel stepped in and pushed the dude. "Back the fuck up," Marcel told him, "she clearly ain't trying to talk to you man."

The dude swung and clipped Marcel on the temple. The punch wobbled Marcel's legs a little, so he pushed the dude again while regaining his balance. The dude threw another punch, but narrowly missed. Marcel returned fire with a hook shot to the dude's cheekbone. That punch sent the dude backwards a few feet. These were two big guys, and people were bouncing off them as they went back and forth in the crowd. They had already cleared out a large section of the floor before security came rushing in.

Right as three security guards arrived, the big White dude landed a quick jab to Marcel's eye. Two of the security guards gang-tackled Marcel, while the other one attempted to calm the big dude down. The security guards were trying to pin Marcel down. Trav and I rushed in and started to pull them off of him.

"Get the fuck off of him!" I yelled. The other security guard came from behind and bear-hugged me. One of the guards that was on top of Marcel popped up and started tussling with Trav.

"Backup motherfucker!" he demanded, "You guys are out of here." Trav's eyes got big and crazy.

"Watch yourself dude," he calmly said. "You sure you wanna do this jo?" The security guard put his hands up and paused. Trav's demeanor made him think twice. "Alright then, come on," the security guard replied, "just head for the door and we'll be cool."

I struggled to free myself, as security started to pull me toward the door. Marcel wrestled his way back to his feet and broke free. "Calm the fuck down!" he demanded, "We fitting to leave. Don't make me go off in this motherfucker!" All of the guards eased up and escorted us out of the club.

When we got outside, we saw the big White dude on the sidewalk. The front door bouncer and another security guard were stopping him from reentering the club. "I'm just trying to talk to my girl bro," the big dude said. "Just let me back in for a minute." He was clearly drunk and not fully understanding the situation. "Stay away from my girl!" he told Marcel.

"Shut the fuck up dude!" Marcel responded. "You ain't fitting to do shit. We can finish this anytime, jo."

A couple of the security guards pleaded with us. "Let it go," one of them said. "Just move down the sidewalk a little. We need to put some space between you guys." Trav stepped right into the security guard's face. "I'll get my boy to back up, but you need to stop putting your hands on people," Trav said. "You dudes is the ones that need to calm down." The security guards backed up. Trav corralled Marcel and we took a few steps down the sidewalk.

"Why you dudes jump on my boy like that?" I asked the security guards, "Why didn't you tackle this motherfucker?" I was pointing at the big White dude.

"Look bro, we're just doing our jobs," one of the security guards replied.

"That's some bullshit jo," I responded.

The big dude charged toward me and the security guards jumped in his path. They pulled him back while he was trying to get at me. "I'll fucking kill you bro!" he yelled at me.

"You're a lame, man," I told him. "You're doing all of this over a girl that ain't even trying to talk to you." He went crazy again and it took all of the security guards just to restrain him.

Before we knew it, a marked police car pulled up. Two White male officers hopped out and approached the security guards. We attempted to discreetly walk away, hoping to slip out of sight before the cops started asking questions. One of the security guards started pointing at us and yelling. At that moment, another marked police car pulled up next to us. We clearly missed our opportunity to avoid interacting with the police. A couple of security guards escorted us back to the front of the club. Two more cops exited their car and joined the scene. Both officers were male, one was White, and the other was Latino.

"Why did you dudes call the police?" Marcel said to the security guards. "That's a weak-ass move. Now this shit is turning into something bigger than it needed to be."

The lead officer and one of the security guards stepped onto the street. We couldn't hear what they were saying, but it was clear that the security guard was explaining what happened. After hearing the security guard's version of the story, the lead officer commanded the other cops to detain all of us. Two of the cops placed Marcel, Trav, and me on one of the police cars. The other officer led the big White dude to the back of the second car. One of the officers gathered our IDs to run our information. When he asked the big dude for his ID, he was met with some resistance.

"Call my uncle," the big dude replied, "he's a captain! He'll be really fucking pissed if you guys arrest me." He went on to say his uncle's name and what district he worked in. I don't remember what he said, but it was a very typical Irish name. "Look, it doesn't matter who your uncle is," the lead cop informed him. "Give the officer your ID right now or you're going straight to jail." The big dude reluctantly pulled his ID out of his wallet and handed it to the cop.

"Look, right there!" he said. "We have the same last name. I'll get his number. It's in my phone bro." The officers ignored his request and they began to search all of us.

The female, who unintentionally became the catalyst of the fight, exited the club. After seeing the scene out front, she quickly became extremely angry with the big White dude.

"Look at what you did," she told him, "you're fucking crazy. Don't ever speak to me again." She got into his face as he was being searched. The lead officer backed her up and commanded that she keep her distance.

"I just wanted to talk," the big dude told her.

"I broke up with you two months ago. We've got nothing to talk about. You're a creep, bro. Just move on," she shot back.

The lead officer stopped his search of the big dude and approached the girl. "You need to calm down," he told her. "Just hold on a minute and I'll get your story, but I don't want to hear another word until then."

The individual searches produced nothing illegal, so the officers started asking questions. We told our version of the events that had transpired. "That's not what the security guards are saying. They're saying that you threw the first punch," said the lead officer, pointing at Marcel.

"What!" Marcel shouted. He took a couple of steps toward the security guards and the cops pulled him back.

"Why you dudes lying?" he asked the security guards. "You just saying that because you guys tackled me down. Now you gotta make it seem like I started this shit."

The security guards stood tall with their arm crossed.

"That's what we saw," one of them replied. "Plus look at his face and you don't even have a mark on you."

In that situation, Marcel's complexion had become a factor in a way he wouldn't have ever expected. At night, under the streetlights. Marcel's brown skin didn't appear to have taken any damage. On the other hand, the big White dude had a very pale skin tone. He had a large knot on his cheekbone and it was turning purple.

"I was just talking to my girlfriend and this guy started throwing punches," the big dude announced. "I don't even know what set him off." The girl at the center of the action demanded to be heard.

"He's lying! He started the whole thing. He was mad because he saw me talking with a guy," she countered.

The lead officer wanted to hear what the big dude had to say about that.

"She's just saying that, because she's mad at me," he responded. "She wants to see me go to jail or something. I swear I didn't throw the first punch."

The police officers had heard enough. They huddled up and discussed their next move. After making a decision, the lead officer announced that Marcel and the big dude were both being placed under arrest.

"Please!" the big dude pleaded, "Just let me call my uncle." The lead officer signaled to the big dude to be quiet. The police handcuffed both of them but placed them in different cars. The big dude was sitting in the back of the lead officer's car. They told everyone to clear out of the area, including Trav and me.

"We got you jo," I shouted to Marcel. "I'm gonna come post your bond fam."

Trav and I walked down the street, back toward where I parked my car. We took it slow, just trying to shake off the preceding chaos. We stopped under the L train tracks, where we bought some waters from a hot dog cart and chilled for a few minutes. Right as we were leaving, we saw a cop car pull up across the street and stop at the entrance to the train platform. A police officer hopped out of the passenger side to open the back door and let someone out. It was the big White dude. The police were letting him walk. He shook the cop's hand and yelled "thanks guys" and he headed up the stairs.

We stayed in the shadows until the police car took off. Neither of us were interested in pressing our luck. Trav was extremely angry about what we just saw. "That's some motherfucking bullshit jo!" he vented. "Dude started the whole thing and now he's just hopping on the train. On his way home and shit. They some crooked motherfuckers."

I was pissed, but not surprised at all.

"That how they operate, man," I said. "They the biggest gang in the city. They ain't gonna lock up one of their own guys." That knowledge didn't make the reality easier to digest though. The big dude started the fight, needed to be restrained multiple times outside the club, and gave the police officers a bunch of attitude. Yet he was walking away clean.

We made it back to the car and headed to my place. I told Trav that he could crash on my couch if he wanted to. We were hoping to get Marcel out of lockup as soon as possible. After a couple of hours, we still hadn't heard from him. I called the precinct and they didn't have his name in the system yet. We both fell asleep while waiting to hear something.

On Sunday morning, I called the precinct again. They had Marcel's name in the system, but they had not set a bail amount for him. "It looks like he has to go before a judge before receiving a bond," they told me, "which means he is going to be bused to The County and have a bond hearing on Monday morning."

They gave me a different phone number to call on Monday. Trav and I were surprised that Marcel was being sent to The County. The expected charges for a fist fight would not typically require a judge to set the bond.

On Monday afternoon, I learned that Marcel's bond was set at fifty thousand dollars. Ten percent of that amount was needed for his release. I knew that Marcel didn't have anyone in his life that had five thousand dollars to spare. I assumed that Marcel was going to be sitting in The County until his court date. I gave Trav a call and filled him in on the situation. We figured that there must have been more to the story if his bail was set that high.

A couple weeks had passed and we still hadn't heard from Marcel. Trav and I decided that we needed to go visit him in The County. I called the hotline in order to find out which building he was being housed in. We went up to The County on his building's next visitation day. We filled out the paperwork, got searched, and were taken to a waiting room. The place was completely packed and we knew that we were going to be there for a while. They finally called us up and gave us a window number. We sat in front of the thick glass and waited for Marcel.

He was shaking his head as he approached the other side of the window. He sat down and picked up the telephone.

"You ain't fitting to believe this shit!" he announced. I figured we'd exchange some basic greetings, but he jumped right into the story.

"They got me in here for the fight, but they added battery against an officer. The cops at the precinct did me dirty, jo." In his anger, he paused and balled up his fists.

"I started talking a lot of shit while they was processing me," he continued. "I was telling them to let me go and shit, because it was just a little fight, it wasn't that big of a deal, but they was just ignoring me. I was still so heated about how that night went down. So, I was thinking 'fuck it, I'm gonna get some shit off my chest,' I told them that they was some pawns. They was just some suckers. Following orders like some Nazis and shit. Trying to destroy an entire group of people. I told them that they minds was all twisted up. How they wasn't able to see right from wrong. I was really pissing them motherfuckers off." He was talking so quickly that he had to stop and catch his breath.

"They was mad, so they put the cuffs back on me while I was being processed," Marcel continued. "They were being all aggressive with me and they put them cuffs on too tight. Two of them cops walked me back to the lockup. We was going down a little hallway and one of them motherfuckers tripped me. My hands was cuffed behind my back. I fell straight onto my face. On the concrete floor. I landed right on my mouth. I think I was knocked out for a few seconds. I straight up broke one of my teeth." Marcel opened his mouth and showed us his cracked tooth.

"I didn't even know they charged me with battery against the police until the judge told me," he said, resuming the story. "I guess they saying I attacked them. They just made some shit up to explain why my tooth got knocked out." Trav and I sympathized with his situation, but it was hard to come up with any encouraging words.

Marcel was clearly in a jam and I couldn't see how he was going to get out of it. The police had made an accusation that is extremely difficult to defend against. It was Marcel's word versus the police officers' word.

After leaving the jail, Trav and I both felt bad about the whole deal. That entire month, we had been chilling as some free men and Marcel was going through hell in the system. He was facing real time and the only thing he was guilty of was running his mouth. The police had exacted double the revenge on him. Not only had they tripped a man who was handcuffed, they falsely charged him with a felony. On a night when he just wanted to get on stage and rap, his life got flipped upside down.

I've always been the type to find a way to fix stuff, but Marcel's situation felt unfixable. The nature of the charges had him backed into a corner. I couldn't imagine how a lawyer could even help his cause with that case.

"Nothing's more powerful than the truth," as the saying goes, but when you're charged with battery against a police officer, the truth isn't worth anything.

I never considered telling Marcel that he didn't stand a chance in court, because hope was worth more than anything at that point. We also didn't tell him that we saw the big White dude get set free. Trav and I had discussed it before we entered the jail. That information would have just made him more frustrated, so we had decided we'd tell him after he was released.

A month later, Marcel took the prosecutor's deal and was sent to prison. He was a changed man when he got released. He began to live his life as though it was him versus the world. He knew that the felony on his record limited his opportunities and his actions became more and more reckless.

A couple of years later, Marcel was murdered. He was shot with over a dozen bullets. I wasn't going to assume how his life would have turned out if he hadn't been so beaten down by the system, but I was certain that the police changed his life deeply with their abuse of power.

10

WILD HUNDREDS HALFWAY HOUSE

In the winter of 2007, I was in the studio working on an instrumental. My cell phone began to vibrate on my desk. It displayed a number that I didn't recognize. I answered the call and Zoeski was on the other end. He had been released from prison that morning.

I was shocked to hear his voice. It had been years since we last spoke. I popped out of my chair and got all pumped up. I was happy for him. He was excited to be 'back in the world.' He had spent most of the day on a bus back to Chicago. His mom had moved into a new apartment while he was locked up, and he was staying there with her. Zoeski was a free man, but not entirely.

He was granted parole and placed on temporary house arrest. A parole officer was coming to see him the next day. He was required to wear an ankle monitor and was not allowed to leave the apartment without permission from his parole officer. He was required to take a drug test once a week; Zoeski had been freed from prison, but his freedom was very much limited. That night, he wasn't concerned with the obstacles of being on parole. Being confined to an apartment felt much better than being behind bars.

"What do you want me to bring you?" I asked him. "Whatever you need, jo. I've got you man." All he wanted was a couple of fifty-pound dumbbells. "You must've got kind of swole in there," I said. "You're just throwing fifty pounders around like that now?"

"I put on a little muscle over the years," he told me. "You know, there's not that much else to do up in there."

A couple of nights later I went to see him. His mom had moved into a high-rise near downtown, so parking spots were scarce. I ended up walking a couple of blocks with fifty pounds in each hand, and by the time I reached his building, I felt like I had gotten a decent workout in. I was excited to see him, but I felt bad about not going to visit him in prison. He had been incarcerated way down in southern Illinois, at least a five-hour drive from Chicago. Throughout those years I had told myself things like, "This month isn't good, but I'll try and go next month." I wished I had just gone and seen him, instead of putting it off over and over.

When he opened the door, I barely recognized him. When he went to jail, he was just a skinny kid. He came out of prison a huge muscular man. He looked just like a running back in the NFL. There was a completely different person standing in front of me. Physical fitness is one of the only positive things about a prison sentence. At least he had taken full advantage of one of his few opportunities.

We hung out for a while. He was surprised by how much technology had advanced in just a few years. Phones were better and televisions got bigger. I did my best to bring him up to date on things. He couldn't wait to hear all of the music that had been released while he was away. He pulled out a bunch of notebooks, each of them full of lyrics he had written while incarcerated. He talked about getting in the studio to record some songs, but he wasn't able to leave the apartment.

"Don't trip man," I told him, "I can bring the studio to you now." At the time he went away to prison, I had a big computer and a bunch of bulky gear. That was over two years earlier, and computers had improved immensely. I could fit everything I needed to record vocals in one bag. This information made his day. I gave him a CD with some of my new beats on it. He was happy to have something to focus on. Sitting around an apartment didn't provide him with many opportunities.

A week later, I brought my recording gear over to his place. He couldn't believe that my laptop could get the job done. We recorded some verses in the living room, finally putting him back in front of the microphone. Aside from building up his muscles, he had spent years sitting around with his life on pause, and he seemed relieved just to get something accomplished.

After a few weeks, Zoeski was feeling the frustration of being on parole. He told me how his parole officer was a tyrant. The officer demanded that he cut his cornrows off and have his tattoos removed. Zoeski had been growing his hair for about six years at that point, and he really didn't want to cut it off because of some dated stereotype. His parole officer claimed that his hair and tattoos made him look like a criminal. His PO was continually threatening to send him back to prison if he didn't comply.

He was equally concerned about the parole officer's need to make a scene.

"My PO is coming over here and yelling at me in the hallway, so everyone on this floor can hear it," he told me, "telling me that I'm probably going back to prison any day now. The neighbors are popping their heads out to see what's going on. They all looking at me crazy."

He had no power in that situation. He felt like his parole officer was out to get him and there was nothing he could do about it. He was seriously considering asking if he could just go back to prison. He felt like it would be easier to serve out the rest of his sentence. He had been correct in his concern about the scenes that his PO was making. Multiple neighbors had made complaints, and a couple of weeks later he was kicked out of his mom's building. Since his name wasn't on the lease, they were legally allowed to make him leave. He was forced to move into a halfway house on the South Side.

A week or so later, I drove way down to 110th Street and Wentworth Ave to see him. I brought him some food and a few things from Walgreens. When I arrived at the front door, an old guy asked me for a cigarette. I gave him one. "I'm here to see Lorenzo," I told him.

He invited me inside and he went upstairs to get Zoeski. I felt depressed the second I walked into that house. There were spots where the carpet was worn down to the floorboards. There were stains on the walls that looked like they had been there since the 80s.

He came down the stairs. His hair was cut down to a tight fade. "It don't feel right man," he said. "I feel like Sampson or something. I lost some of my powers."

We went and hung out on the front porch. He told me how his parole officer had given him a twenty-four-hour ultimatum. If he didn't cut his hair, then he was going back to the joint. He decided he didn't want to find out if his PO was bluffing or not. I never thought that his parole officer would've taken the threat that far.

I gave Zoeski the bag of items he had requested. He pulled out a marker and wrote his name on everything. "A bunch of these guys in this house are dopeheads trying to get off that shit," he told me. "Most of them got some really sticky fingers, jo. I've got to mark everything that's mine. I can't believe I got stuck living with these dudes!"

I also brought him a couple of CDs to listen to. One CD was full of songs he had requested. The other contained a bunch of my hip hop instrumentals. He wanted to hear the instrumentals immediately. My car was parked on the curb, right in front of the house. His ankle monitor allowed him to go one hundred feet from the box. My car was within that distance, so we hopped in. We were going through the beats and talking. He was just happy to be sitting in a car and listening to music. I was reminding myself to be more grateful for everything I had, because sitting in a parked car was the highlight of Zoeski's day.

About twenty minutes later, I saw some headlights coming toward us down the street. We were sitting on 110th Street, which is a one-way. The car was traveling the wrong way, against traffic. This meant that either someone had made a wrong turn, or it was the police.

I knew this because the cops sometimes like to drive the opposite way down one-way streets. First of all, no one's going to give them a ticket: they could get away with it, so it was just another way to show everybody they were above the rules. From a strategic standpoint, this also allows them to stop traffic and create an unofficial check point.

As the car got closer to us, I could see that it was the police. It was an unmarked car, but it had a big black push bumper on the front grill, which instantly made me nervous: only the police drive around with push bumpers. They were clearly on the hunt. They drove by and stared right at us. I thought we were good, because they kept on going. Then they stopped and reversed their car back up the block.

"Oh fuck jo!" Zoeski shouted. "Them detectives are on us."

The cops pulled up next to us and shined their spotlight right into our eyes. They pulled forward and parked on the curb behind my car. They didn't wait for any backup. Two detectives jumped out of the unmarked car like they couldn't wait to speak with us. One detective came to my window and the other went to Zoeski's side.

Both of them were young White guys. I was surprised. I had never seen two cops partnered together that both looked so young. Typically, the police pair an older officer with a younger one. I was even more surprised by the fact that both of these guys had made the rank of detective at their age. Neither of them appeared to be over thirty years old.

The detective on my side had blondish hair and a pale complexion. The guy at Zoeski's window was dark haired with an olive skin tone. They were both extremely muscular, to the extent that their physiques may have been chemically enhanced. The blonde cop had a big grin on his face, while the other guy had a serious mean mug. I figured we were in for a good cop/bad cop routine.

"Why the fuck are you guys sitting in this car?" The blonde detective said, "What are you, a couple of faggots or something?" He loudly laughed at his own joke, like a kid in middle school. I was wrong about the good cop/bad cop assumption. The grin on the blonde cop's face wasn't because he was friendly. He was just a cocky douchebag. I figured that he had made an easy transition from Catholic high school bully to the Chicago Police Department.

Neither of us answered his stupid question. I just gave him a look that said, "come on, man." His grin quickly disappeared and they asked to see our IDs. The blonde cop read my address. "That's way over on the West Side," he said, "what are you doing all the way down here?"

"I'm visiting my friend," I told him. "He just moved into that house right there."

"I know that place," he said. "That's a halfway house." He popped his head into my window.

"What are you a dopehead or something?" he asked Zoeski.

"Naw man, I'm just in a bad situation right now," Zoeski answered. The detectives both laughed.

"Yeah right, that's what every dopehead says," the blonde cop jabbed. "Why don't both of you get out of the car and we'll figure this all out." I wasn't sure what they had to figure out, because we weren't breaking any laws. But I knew from experience that the law had nothing to do with the situation at hand.

Both detectives pulled their guns out of their holsters. They kept their guns lowered.

"Put your hands on your head and keep them there," the dark-haired cop commanded.

The detectives opened the doors and we slowly got out of the car. My phone was sitting on my lap. As I stood up, the phone fell onto the street. They raised their guns, then walked us over to the hood of their car and we assumed the position. When they put their guns back on their waists, I felt relieved. I was legitimately nervous for a few seconds. They looked like they wanted to pull the triggers. I felt like they had some unexplained personal beef with us. It wasn't like some older cops, bullying a couple of kids; those guys were the same age as me and it felt like they had something to prove.

They began to search us. The dark-haired detective was patting down Zoeski's pants. He got down to his ankles. "What's this?" he asked.

"I'm on house arrest," Zoeski answered. "That's my ankle monitor."

"What are you on house arrest for?" the blonde cop asked, jumping into the conversation.

"I got into some trouble and I'm just paying for that right now," Zoeski replied.

"You know you're not allowed to be out here sitting in this fucking car, right?" the blonde cop informed him. "You just violated your house arrest."

"I'm within one hundred feet of the box," Zoeski said, "I'm not violating right now."

"Once you got into the car, you were in violation," the detective declared. "It doesn't matter how far you are from the box. You might not have triggered a notification, but you're not allowed to be sitting in a car on the street."

"No one told me that," Zoeski pleaded. "Ayy man, I wasn't doing nothing."

"Yeah well, we'll see how this goes," replied the detective.

The blonde cop finished searching me. "Your fucking story isn't adding up," he said.

"There's not much to add up," I replied. "I drove down here to see my friend and bring him a few things. That's it."

"Yeah, but what were you bringing him?" he said. "You came down here from the West Side. Odds are, you're bringing some dope to sell."

I will admit, I was happy to not be labeled as a dopehead. Being accused of selling drugs felt much less demeaning. That night, Zoeski was the one who had to deal with the dopehead label.

"I'm not selling any drugs," I informed him. "I've got nothing on me bro."

He got angry and slammed me into the push bumper. My stomach hit right on the bar and I thought I was going to vomit. I was in some serious pain, but I was trying my best not to let him know.

"I'm not your fucking bro!" he shouted, "I'm not friends with motherfuckers like you."

He drove his weight on me, making it hard to breath. I knew I should have addressed him as "officer," but I was finding it hard to muster up any respect for that guy.

"Alright, I hear you," I struggled to speak. "Please just ease up." He immediately pulled me off of the car. I was pretty sure that he just needed to hear me beg. His ego seemed to be appeased the second I said 'please.'

"We'll see what you've got in the car," he said. He nodded his head toward my car and the dark-haired cop began the search.

"Why are you two friends?" the blonde cop asked me. "Do you think you're Black or something?" I knew he was trying to provoke me in order to escalate the situation. It seemed like he was itching to throw a punch.

"Wait what? I'm not Black?" I said. "Are you sure?"

I couldn't help myself. I assumed I was about to get punched, slammed, or handcuffed. Instead, he started laughing. "You're fucking funny huh?" he said. "Okay, you can have that one."

The dark-haired detective finished searching the passenger's side of my car. He proceeded to the driver's side and began to poke around. I could see my phone was sitting right next to his boot.

"My phone fell out of the car. It's right there by your feet," I told him. "Can you grab it for me? I just don't want you to accidentally step on it."

He pointed his flashlight down and saw the phone there.

"I see it," he responded. "Yeah, I wouldn't want to step on it." Then he stomped my phone into the pavement a couple of times. "Sorry. My foot slipped."

I didn't say a word. I just shook my head and looked away. I've always been very careful with my things, and I didn't have insurance on that phone. When I made the decision to not get the insurance plan. I hadn't factored in a detective purposefully destroying it. Just like that I was out a couple hundred dollars.

He continued to search the car and found nothing illegal. The blonde cop instructed him to run our IDs. The two detectives looked the same age, but the blonde guy clearly had more rank. He appeared to be hazing his own partner, like they were in a fraternity. About five minutes later, the dark-haired cop emerged from the car. He pointed to me and said, "This guy is clean."

Then he looked at Zoeski.

"But this fucking guy isn't just on house arrest, he's on parole." He proceeded to slam Zoeski onto the hood and held him there.

"You've got some felonies you piece of shit," he continued. "You're fucked now."

"I figured you had that ankle monitor because you had a DUI or something," the blonde cop said. "Put some cuffs on him." The dark-haired detective handcuffed Zoeski very aggressively.

"You don't need to do this," Zoeski informed him. "I've been doing everything they've been asking me to do. I've been good. I promise you."

"I don't really give a fuck," the blonde guys answered. "I bet one of you stashed some drugs when we rolled by."

"We're clean man," Zoeski responded. "You just searched us." The dark-haired cop slammed him on the car again.

"Shut the fuck up!" he yelled. "Save it for your PO." He pulled Zoeski off of the hood and placed him in the back of their car.

"Ayy come on," I told the blonde detective. "We didn't do nothing wrong. They're going to send him back to prison if you guys take him in. Can't you just let him slide this time?" He looked me dead in the eyes.

"Just get the fuck out of here," he told me. "I swear If I ever see you again, I'll make sure you go to jail." I couldn't argue with that. I grabbed my belongings off of the hood and nodded to Zoeski. I figured I wasn't going to see him for a while.

The detectives flicked their lights on and sped off. I grabbed my cell phone off of the pavement and jumped in my car. I inspected the phone. I hoped that it hadn't been completely destroyed, because it held a lot of information that wasn't backed up. My hope died quickly when I saw that the screen was shattered into pieces and it wouldn't start up. I threw it on the seat and headed for the expressway.

I was feeling some guilt as I drove home. I knew that it wasn't my fault, but I felt bad about how everything went down. Zoeski was on his way to jail and I was going home to my bed. We were in the wrong place at the wrong time. Those two detectives were out looking for some action and we just happened to be sitting ducks.

Experiencing the events of that night as a twenty-nine-year-old, I processed them in a new way. I didn't have as many personal emotions toward those detectives. I wasn't dreaming up a scenario that would give me an opportunity for revenge. The blonde cop went out of his way to belittle us, but that part didn't bother me very much. I knew exactly what he was doing and that enabled me to not feel his words.

I wasn't concerned about my own feelings that time around. I was mostly thinking about how those two psychos were on the streets with the law on their side. I knew that everyone in their jurisdiction was in danger.

I felt bad about how everything had played out for Zoeski. The excitement of his prison release was short-lived. He felt like a free man until he met his PO. His parole officer took every opportunity available to bully him. Zoeski made a deal and cut his hair off in order to stay out of jail. That deal only lasted a matter of days until it was voided by another couple of bullies.

All of this made me ask myself how anyone in Zoeski's position could ever trust authority. In his short time out of prison, he felt the pain of multiple officers using their powers sadistically. I wondered how many people chose a career in law enforcement just for the power.

In my opinion, not all people with authority have bad intentions, but those with bad intentions are drawn to high levels of authority. This is one of the biggest problems in the state of law enforcement.

My mind began to fill with questions about who the police were, as individuals. I had always viewed them as a group, but dealing with officers my own age changed my point of view. I really began to theorize why people become officers of the law.

I feel like a lot of cadets have good intentions and want to help others. They view the role of officer as something righteous and see an opportunity to effectuate positive change. Unfortunately, the culture they enter into changes idealistic young recruits into ethically compromised officers.

Some individuals simply view it as a job that they are technically qualified for. Some people have personal connections that create a simple path. For them, it is a way to earn a living and receive great benefits. I have heard police officers say, "It's just another job. I clock in and I clock out," and "I didn't know what else to do, so I became a cop." That sounds alright at first, but it truly is a significant issue, and law enforcement is unlike any other profession: it has too much of an impact on society to be viewed as just a paycheck.

The power that is immediately bestowed upon an officer of the law is unique. That level of power creates unparalleled opportunities for corruption. If an individual has chosen this profession as a source of income, they are much more likely to be tempted by the gains of corruption. Whether they rob people or arrest people on bogus charges, they are not only supplementing their income, but they are advancing their career. There is too much on the line for law enforcement to be viewed as "just another job."

After that night, it became more than evident to me. The police behaved in an entirely different manner in Black neighborhoods. Those two young detectives became just another example of this fact. They were out looking for trouble, and when they didn't find any, they were more than willing to make some trouble. They had been aggressive and demeaning from the very start: they had chosen to inflict physical pain on both Zoeski and me; we hadn't even provoked their violence; they were obviously looking to dish out some abuse and we became their targets. I had never seen that type of behavior outside of a Black neighborhood—the average American is not aware of how drastic the situation is.

To this day, even with all the video evidence of extreme police misconduct that has surfaced in more recent years, I believe the majority of people still do not realize the level of police oppression that occurs on a day-to-day basis.

As for Zoeski, the detectives ended up charging him. This prompted his parole officer to declare him in violation of the conditions of his parole. He spent a couple of weeks in The County before getting shipped back to the penitentiary. Zoeski served out the remaining time on his sentence. He wrote me a letter informing me how he wished he had never been paroled. The pressure and stress that his parole officer had put on him was more difficult to deal with than being locked up.

11

IMPOUNDED IN HOLLYWOOD

In 2008, I made a decision to expand my music production reach. Up until that time, I had exclusively been working on urban music. I had worked with many singers, but every instrumental I had created was categorically hip hop. I really wanted to give myself the opportunity to work with as many artists as possible. Through a friend of a friend, I was introduced to a classically trained pianist named Adam. His knowledge of music theory was far beyond my own. At that time, I knew the basics of music theory—enough to compose an instrumental—but I often played the keyboard by ear. After a couple of studio sessions, Adam and I decided to team up and make some tracks together.

As a production duo, we could confidently work in any genre of music, and we wanted to take a shot at the big money. We focused on making Top 40-style pop instrumentals. We passed our music on to Tay-O, who knew a few gifted singers and songwriters. Tay-O had made a lot of relationships in Los Angeles and was spending a significant amount of time out there. In 2009, I flew to LA a few times to get some songs recorded. By the spring of 2010, I was frequently traveling back and forth between Los Angeles and Chicago.

I decided to get a place in Hollywood so I could make more connections in the industry. All I needed was a spot to sleep and somewhere to work on my computer. I found a little studio apartment right off of Sunset Boulevard.

A few weeks after I moved in, Tay-O needed to borrow my SUV so he could move some large items. He came over and we traded automobiles. I thought nothing of it at the time. Around eleven PM, Tay-O called me. He was at the Los Angeles Police Department Wilshire Station. He asked me to pick him up and he would explain everything when I got there. I jumped in Tay-O's car and headed down to Venice Blvd. When I pulled up, Tay-O was sitting on a bench out front. He looked stressed out as he got into the car. "Ayy, don't you want to drive?" I asked him, as I started to get out of the driver's seat.

"Naw man, you can drive," he responded, "I'm too Black to be driving around here."

I was wondering where my truck was and what was going on, but I went ahead and pulled off. I didn't want to sit in front of the police station, so I pulled into a convenience store parking lot so Tay-O could fill me in on the situation.

"Man, I didn't even make it five blocks from your crib bro," Tay-O said. "The police seen me drive by and they got right behind me. They pulled me over a few seconds later. They seen me in that truck and I guess they couldn't resist. The cops kept asking me if there were any drugs in the vehicle." I owned a black Cadillac Escalade at the time. Tay-O felt like the police profiled him as a drug dealer because he was a Black man driving a nice truck.

"Why did they pull you over though?" I asked him.

"I asked them why and they said that there had been some cars stolen in the area recently," Tay-O replied. "That wasn't the first time I've heard that bullshit reason before." His story was the epitome of racial targeting.

The police saw a Black guy that caught their attention, and they gave a vague excuse for pulling him over.

"Yeah, I hear ya, but where is my truck man?" I impatiently asked.

"I'm about to get there fam," Tay-O said with a smile. "They asked for the registration and insurance. I told them that I had just borrowed the truck from you, so I needed to check the usual spots. Once I said that, them dudes told me to get out of the vehicle. The cop on the shotgun side upped his pistol and pointed that shit right at my dome. The motherfucking LAPD be so goddamn jumpy like that."

Tay-O stopped to clear his throat and I motioned to him to keep telling the story. I was still waiting to hear what happened to my truck.

"Man jo, I'm dying of thirst over here," he continued. "Let's go up in this store real quick." I laughed, because I knew that he was enjoying fucking with me a little bit. I understood where he was coming from though. Dealing with the police always seemed to dehydrate me too. After we grabbed some waters, Tay-O got back to the story.

"One of them cops was searching me as the other one started searching the truck," he continued. "The dude searching the car said that he couldn't find the registration anywhere. I asked them to just let me call you, so you could come and get your truck. The cop that was searching me had taken my wallet and cellphone. He went to run the plates, to see if the truck was reported stolen. I kept telling them that I could clear the shit up if they just let me call you. They weren't interested in that, though. They just wanted to book me for something and impound the truck. They took me to the police station and held me till I called you. They was waiting to see if the truck was gonna get reported stolen. Finally, they gave up and let me go."

"They impounded my truck?" I clarified.

"Yeah man, they called for a tow truck to come get your shit," Tay-O replied.

"Fuck man, let's go get it then!" I said.

"They told me that the lot doesn't open up till the morning," he answered. "Plus, you gonna have to go back to the police station and fill out some paperwork. They said you need to bring the title and registration."

"But the registration card is in the truck," I said.

"That's not what they was saying," Tay-O replied. "They gave me a ticket with a court date, because there was no paperwork in the vehicle."

"I just got the registration paper earlier today," I responded. "Then I went up to the insurance office and got all that shit taken care of. Oh fuck dude!"

I started searching through my pockets. I pulled out both cards from my back pocket. I forgot to put them in the glove compartment.

"My bad family," I apologized. "I can't believe I had this shit in my pocket the whole time!"

I had been a little irritated with Tay-O, because of the inconvenience. Then I felt like an asshole, because it was all my fault. The fact that he got held at the police station and got a ticket was on me.

The police pulling Tay-O over for no reason was on them, though. They created a series of events that ended up costing both Tay-O and me some time and money. It was a situation that could have easily been resolved if they just acted like reasonable human beings. I had been pulled over only once in all the years that I owned that truck. I was speeding and I received a ticket without a personal or vehicle search. A Black man driving the same truck didn't even travel a mile before getting racially targeted and searched by the police.

Tay-O ended up sleeping on my couch that night. In the morning, we went back to the police station and then to the impound lot. I ended up paying over one hundred dollars to get my truck out. I had to take that loss at a time when my funds were very tight. Fortunately, I had the money. It really made me think about all the people who just didn't have it.

Every day a car sits in the pound the price to reclaim it increases, and it becomes less likely that a person without much money will ever see it again. They may not have done anything wrong, but they can still end up losing their car essentially because a police officer is looking to show productivity and create revenue. Moreover, if the car isn't claimed, the police will sell it for profit.

12

LONG BEACH BOSS MAN

Over the next six months, I spent a lot of my time working with songwriters and trying to network. I had made some good connections, but I knew that I needed to continue pursuing every available opportunity. A songwriter I was working with introduced me to a guy named Claude. His nickname was "Tiger Claw," a play on his name, but he simply went by TC. She told me that he was a 'baller' and that he was looking for a good producer to work with.

TC was a Haitian dude from Miami. He had a record label there and worked with several artists in South Florida. TC would often travel to LA in order to promote the singers and rappers he represented. Like everyone in Los Angeles, he was constantly looking to broaden his industry connections and searching for any new avenues. He definitely had the vibe of a promoter: nice clothes, expensive watches, and the gift of gab. Every time he flew into town, he would rent a luxury car. He was really into making a memorable first impression on people.

TC and I never really saw eye-to-eye on music, but we became fast friends. In early 2011, he came out to LA for the week. In true Miami-style, he pulled up to my apartment building in the nicest BMW he could get his hands on, and he brought company. He had flown out the top rapper on his label, a young kid named Paulo. I don't remember his stage name, but it was "lil" something or other. He was of Black-Brazilian descent and was working the international angle. TC had finessed a meeting with a music distributor, scheduled for the following morning.

We hung out in Hollywood for a while. I showed Paulo some places that he wanted to visit. That night, TC decided to get a hotel room in Hollywood, so they wouldn't have to travel very far in the morning. They had been staying in Long Beach at a friend's place, so they needed to drive back to pick up their luggage. TC insisted that I ride with them so we could talk some more. He was hoping to get some advice for their meeting. He also wanted me to coach Paulo a little, because he had never been around any executive types before.

Around forty minutes later, we pulled up to a house in North Long Beach. After grabbing their luggage, we headed back toward the 91 freeway. I was sitting in the backseat and I noticed that TC kept looking in his rear-view mirror. He made a right turn and checked his mirror again.

"I think the LAPD is behind us," he said.

"If there's police behind us, then it's the Long Beach Police," I told him, "not the LAPD."

"Are they cooler than the LAPD?" TC asked me.

"No, not really man," I said honestly. "If anything, they're worse."

A year earlier, Tay-O and I had an encounter with the Long Beach Police. They acted like complete jackasses during a bogus stop and search, so I was nervous to hear that they were tailing us. TC just kept driving the speed limit and we saw the sign for the entrance ramp. It felt like we might just make it out of Long Beach without any problems.

Right before we could pull onto the ramp, the police turned their lights on. Without a safe place to pull over, TC drove past the ramp and found a good spot on the shoulder of the road. We sat there and waited for a while, so I figured the police were running the license plate. It was a rental car, so that wasn't any concern for us.

"We rode past them a few minutes ago," TC said. "They were pulling out of a parking lot and I could see them looking right at us." A few minutes later, a backup squad car arrived. They pulled behind the other cop car.

"Oh shit dog!" Paulo said. "There's more cops now. What the fuck? We didn't do nothing!"

TC and I remained relatively calm, but Paulo, who was only twenty at the time, was getting very jumpy. The officers who pulled us over finally approached our vehicle. Both officers were males, in their thirties or early forties. The lead cop came to TC's side. He was a light-haired White guy with a crewcut. The other officer, who covered the passenger side, was Latino. They both had their guns out and lowered as they came to the windows. They kept some distance and held their position while the backup officers circled around to the front of the car. Their tactical maneuvers felt a bit over-the-top for a traffic stop, so I figured they were looking to do more than simply write a speeding ticket or something.

"Everyone in the vehicle, put your hands on your head," the lead cop demanded. We were confused, but we followed his orders. "Driver! Slowly exit the vehicle," he shouted. TC did just that and they ordered him to lay face down on the asphalt.

"This is a brand-new outfit though," TC pleaded. "Do I really have to get on the ground?"

The lead officer grabbed TC by the arm and pulled him to the pavement. "Put your hands behind your head and don't move!" he ordered.

"Why didn't you pull over immediately?" The lead officer continued. "I was just about to ram you off the road."

"There wasn't anywhere to pull over back there," TC replied.

"You were probably thinking about making a run for it," the lead officer said. "You made the right decision, pulling over. You would've never gotten away in this German piece of crap."

The officers led Paulo and I out of the vehicle and laid us down, next to TC. At that point, I got a good look at the backup officers. One of them was a younger Asian guy and the other was a middle-aged White dude. They began searching Paulo and me. The Asian cop was being very aggressive with Paulo. He had his knee jammed into Paulo's ribs.

"What the fuck dog?" Paulo shouted. "That shit hurts!" The officer moved his knee onto Paulo's spine and put all his weight onto the middle of his back. Paulo let out a loud groan of pain and began to squirm. The lead officer holstered his gun and joined the other cop on Paulo's back.

"Stop resisting!" the lead officer shouted, as he drove Paulo's head into the pavement.

"I'm not resisting!" Paulo replied. The lead officer grabbed Paolo's arms and pulled them behind his back. He proceeded to handcuff Paulo, while they had him pinned down under their knees.

"Stop man!" TC shouted at the lead officer. "He's not fighting. He didn't do nothing." The lead officer drove his knee in one last time as he stood up. Paulo looked like he was holding back tears from the pain. The Asian cop eased up his pressure and that allowed Paulo to catch his breath.

"What is going on man?" TC asked the cops.

"That's what we're trying to figure out," the lead officer answered. He spoke as if we did something to provoke their aggression. I had been through situations like that one before, but I was genuinely confused. Every move the cops had made was extreme and unnecessary. It felt like they had been searching for someone to practice their tactics on. They probably got a look at TC and Paulo's dreadlocks and thought they were perfect candidates.

"What is your reason for pulling us over though?" I said. "You have to have a reason for stopping us."

"Well, there is some drug traffic around here and you guys fit the profile," the lead officer replied. I could not believe he actually admitted that they had profiled us. I had never heard that one before. There was nothing illegal about looking the way we looked.

"That's not cause for stopping and searching us though," I responded. The lead officer got visibly angry and stood directly over me. He jammed his boot between my face and the ground.

"Do you think you are smart?" he said. "I would stop talking if I were you. Just let us do our jobs and don't push it." Considering what they did to Paulo, I decided to shut up.

The officers resumed their search as the lead cop stood over us. His posture was like a boss man, overseeing a chain gang. He had a toothpick hanging off his lip. It took every bit of my resolve to not start laughing at that guy. He might as well have been chewing on a straw of hay.

"Look at this!" the Latino cop shouted, "What do we have here?" He pulled a wad of cash out of TC's pocket. It was around seven or eight hundred dollars.

"Were you planning on making a drug deal with that money?" the lead officer said. "That's a lot of money to be carrying around."

"No officer, that's just my traveling money," TC replied. "We just came out here from Miami a few days ago. We're here on music business. I run a record label and I do some promotions. I have a bunch of business cards in the car." The lead officer shined his flashlight on the rental car.

"Okay Bob Marley," the lead officer laughed and said, "so I'm not going to find any drugs or money in the car?"

"No sir," TC replied.

He began slowly walking around the car. He appeared to be strategizing his next move, but he was hamming it up. It felt like he was performing a scene to the point where I started to look around for movie cameras. It seemed as though he was in an alternate reality, like there was a film playing in his mind.

One of the backup officers collected our IDs and went back to his squad car. The lead officer began to methodically search TC's rental car. The Latino cop began to work a different angle.

"Listen, my partner is a little intense, so watch what you say to him," he whispered to us. "You don't want to set him off. I'm cool though, so you'd rather talk to me." It was clear that he was playing the role of good cop.

"Why do you really have that much money on you?" he continued. "Come on, tell me the truth."

"There's no more to the story," TC answered. "I like having some cash in my pocket when I'm this far from home. I don't really like putting things on credit."

The reality was, TC was just that kind of dude. He was a flashy guy and he always carried a lot of cash. No one would have traveled from Florida to California to make an eight-hundred-dollar drug deal. The angle the police were taking just didn't make any sense.

"We're going to have to search all of these bags," the lead officer said from the trunk area. He called for the middle-aged officer to assist him. They started to tear through TC and Paulo's luggage.

"It's better if you tell me now. Are there any drugs in your bags?" the Latino officer asked. TC quickly shook his head and gave the cop an irritated look. He was clearly tired of hearing the same questions over and over.

"Well I'm trying to work with you, but if you don't want to tell me anything, then there's nothing I can do for you." The cop said.

They abruptly ended their vehicle search and returned into our line of sight. "I can tell that you guys are criminals, but you got lucky tonight," the lead cops informed us. "We don't have any more time for this. Go ahead and clean up the mess. Then you guys can go on your way."

They un-cuffed Paulo and they were gone in under sixty seconds. It was strange; the situation went from very intense to over so quickly. TC and

Paulo were saddened by what we discovered after we collected ourselves. The cops had left their clothes and other belongings scattered on the pavement. A bunch of their clothes were dirty and some of the stuff was clearly stepped on. They were both deflated by seeing their best stuff callously thrown around. After getting everything picked up and put away, TC noticed something.

"Yo, where's my watch?" TC questioned. He said some designer's name.

"I spent almost a stack on that piece!" TC continued. He started searching through everything again. The hasty departure of the police started to make more sense. I assumed that they found something they liked and made a quick getaway. After a while, TC gave up on his search and we took off.

It was a quiet trip back to Hollywood. TC was distraught by everything that went down. I typically would try to find a positive spin on things after the dust settled, not because I was such a positive guy, but I just didn't like wasting time and energy on things that couldn't be fixed. While most things in life could be repaired or at least viewed in a different light, getting robbed and mistreated by the police was not one of them. There was nothing any of us could say or do to even slightly balance the scales.

When we got back to Hollywood, TC dropped me off and they headed straight to their room. They had to be up early in the morning and the Long Beach Police kept us out later than we planned. I talked to TC the following afternoon and he didn't feel very great about their meeting. He thought that Paulo and he hadn't been in a good mental place.

"I ain't going to lie man," he said, "our confidence was a little fucked up. I think that shit with the police got under our skin or something."

That information brought me right back to thoughts from the past. I had wished so many times that the police could just see the consequences of their actions. Some part of me had always hoped that they would change their ways if they only knew. That type of thinking might have been too wishful. As I got older and wiser, I lost that type of hope.

If someone is operating under an ideology of good-guys-versus-bad-guys, it becomes easier to justify any action. If any Black guy driving a nice car is assumed to be a bad guy, then the police can become Dirty Harry; they can bend the rules and still feel like they have the moral high ground.

13

POLITE, RESPECTFUL, AND CORRUPT

In October of 2012, I took a trip to Dallas to visit Tay-O. His girlfriend, Nicole, had taken a job and relocated to Dallas. Tay-O was a free-spirited dude who always possessed the need to get out and see the world; the notion of packing his bags and hopping on a plane did not intimidate him. Nikki had been pleading with him to come and spend some time there, and Tay-O knew a few people and had some family there, so the trip would also present him with some opportunities.

He was born to network. In no time, he had dozens of friends and acquaintances throughout the Dallas-Fort Worth area. His cousin introduced him to a girl who was an aspiring singer. She was nineteen and had some talent. She was looking for a music producer and someone to help with her songwriting. Tay-O always went out of his way to connect people who could benefit from each other.

He told me that he found an artist who I had to meet, insisting that I needed to pack my gear and take a trip. Nikki had an extra bedroom, and I was welcome to stay at her place, so I wouldn't need to spend money on a hotel room. With a free place to stay and a reason to get out of town, I jumped on a plane to DFW with no real plans other than to see an old friend and meet with a potential artistic collaborator.

I had already visited Dallas on multiple occasions, so I was familiar with the place. Like most people I've encountered in the North and on the West Coast, I had originally assumed that Dallas was deep in the heart of Texas, that people spoke with a thick Southern drawl and wore cowboy hats. I learned quickly that Dallas was a progressive American city with just a touch of old Texas. I was excited to visit again, because I had had some good times on previous trips there.

When I arrived, Tay-O was really happy to see me. He had already built a solid social life there, but he wasn't tight with anyone, and he was relieved to have one of his boys from home around. We spent most of the time hanging out in the day and going out at night. I set up a makeshift workspace in the spare bedroom. After a few days, the aspiring singer came over to meet with me. She had a good voice and a unique style, so I could see some potential.

After picking out some tracks that caught her ear, we began to write, but she continually struggled with her melodies and eventually lost her confidence. We ended the day with very little accomplished. I felt like she wasn't quite ready for the studio yet, and any hopes of making some music on that trip were quickly fading.

I was cool with the idea of just hanging out and getting to know Dallas better, though. I realized, after meeting a few of Nikki's friends, that she was attempting to play matchmaker, and had informed all of her single friends that I was coming to town. I had just ended a long relationship a couple of months earlier, so I couldn't complain. I was newly single and happy to meet some fresh faces.

On a Wednesday evening, a friend of Nikki's came over to hang out. I was relaxing on the couch in some basketball shorts and a t-shirt. The second she walked in the door I felt underdressed. She was beautiful and radiated positive energy. I introduced myself and immediately dipped into the bedroom to change my clothes. I reemerged a little fresher and feeling more confident. I felt a real connection developing when I talked to her. We ended up making plans to go out on Friday night. I was normally calm and cool about dating, but she made me a little nervous. I had never felt that level of instant attraction before.

On Friday afternoon Tay-O and I went to meet up with a friend of his, a local dude who went by Big A. He had just bought a place west of Downtown Dallas. He was doing some rehabbing and was excited to show us his work. After talking for a while, Big A asked us if we wanted to take a drive to the south side so he could pick up some tools from his parent's house. I didn't have to be anywhere for a few hours, so I was cool with taking a ride. We got in Tay-O's car and headed for the Interstate. We stopped to get something to eat in the Oak Cliff neighborhood. Big A wanted me to get a taste of some local food. I preferred to eat at local joints when I traveled, so I was happy to grab some Texas BBQ.

It had gotten dark outside while we were eating, and I was itching to get back to Nikki's place so I could get ready for the night. Big A promised he would be in and out of his parent's house. We only had to travel a mile down the road and then we could head back. We made a left turn out of the parking lot. At the next intersection, I saw a police car quickly pull up to the light and hit the brakes hard. We drove by them and I kept my eye on the side mirror to see what they were up to.

The marked police car turned at the light and began to trail us, hanging a few car lengths back. I peeked over at the speedometer and saw that Tay-O was locked in on the speed limit. "You see them, huh?" I said.

"Yeah man, I've been watching them since that light," he replied. "We should be good though. They're just running the plates. When everything comes back clean. They'll probably get off us." Big A was unaware that the cops were behind us. "You saying the police are following us?"

"Yeah, they've been back there," I replied.

"Oh shit!" Big A shouted. "Watch your speed man!"

A few seconds later, we heard the siren and saw the lights whirling. Tay-O pulled over to the side of the road. I had never had an encounter with the Dallas Police Department, so I wasn't sure how to prepare. Two officers got out of the car and covered both sides of our vehicle. They were both White males, the one on the driver's side around fifty years old, the other in his thirties. The older cop took the lead.

"How you all doing?" he asked. "Do you mind getting your license for me?"

Tay-O already had his license ready and handed it over. I immediately felt good about the situation, because the officer was being extremely polite.

"Now I'm going to need you to slowly get the registration," he said. "Tell me now if you have a gun in the glove compartment." Tay-O assured him that there were no guns in the car.

"Alright, but if you're reaching for a gun this is going to end really bad for you," he declared while chuckling. The officer on my side aimed his flashlight at the glove compartment with one hand, with his other hand grabbing the handle of his gun. Tay-O retrieved the registration and gave it to the older cop.

"Can I ask why you pulled us over, officer?" Tay-O inquired.

"You clipped the line back there, when you made that left turn," he answered.

At that point, my feelings about the situation quickly changed. I was certain, without a doubt, that it would have been impossible for them to see such a small detail from that distance. They were almost two blocks away and it was dark outside.

I had been well aware of that tactic long before that night. Numerous friends of mine had been pulled over for 'clipping the line.' Every day there are countless lines being clipped, especially during turns. It is the most ticky-tack traffic infraction that exists. Police can always use the 'clipping the line' excuse if they are interested in pulling a vehicle over without

110

cause.

"Just give me a minute," the older cop said. "I'll make sure everything is in order here and I'll be right back."

The officer was really throwing me off with his behavior. He was clearly full of shit, but he was being so nice about it. I soon realized that he was using politeness as a tool. He was attempting to gain our trust, most likely with the hope that we might simply admit to some wrongdoings. It felt like he was playing a part, like he had a script.

While the lead officer was running the information, the younger cop began to shine his flashlight throughout the car. "Did you just grab something?" he asked Big A. "Let me see your hands."

"I didn't even move." He showed him his palms.

"All of you all, put your hands on your heads and keep them there," the younger officer commanded.

We complied with his demand. He intensified his flashlight search of the interior through the windows. He appeared to be very jumpy and he placed his hand back on the handle of his gun. That made me freeze up. I assumed he was fairly new to the job and more nervous than we were. I wasn't interested in giving him a reason to overreact.

"Everything appears to be good here, so you can go ahead and put the registration back in the glove compartment," said the older officer, returning from his vehicle. "I'm going to hold on to your driver's license for a minute," he told Tay-O.

The situation was clearly developing into more than a petty traffic violation. The older cop leaned over and popped his head through the window.

"Now you all don't have any drugs in the vehicle, do you?" he asked. We assured him that there were no drugs in the car.

"Well, I'm going to need you all to step out of the vehicle for safety concerns," he said.

"We weren't doing anything wrong," Big A replied. "He was just driving me to my parent's house, so I can pick up some tools. It's just down the road."

"Alright, we can talk out here on the side of the road," the officer responded, "where it's safer for everyone."

The officers escorted Tay-O and I to the hood of their car. Meanwhile, Big A was in the backseat continuing to plead his case. After getting me situated, the younger cop removed Big A and placed him on the trunk of Tay-O's car. They began to pat-down Big A and Tay-O.

"All of this is unnecessary," Big A insisted.

He would not stop talking. I just wanted him to shut up because I didn't want him to set them off. Surprisingly, Big A's non-stop chatter didn't seem to annoy either officer. I figured it was a cultural thing. I was in a different part of the country and witnessing some behavior that I wasn't accustomed to.

"Alright, Alright," the older cop replied. "I hear what you're saying. We're just doing our jobs here." My blood boiled and I bit my tongue when he said that. His folksy approach couldn't mask the bullshit. By no means was an unwarranted stop and search part of doing their jobs.

"So where were you all headed tonight?" the older cop asked Tay-O and me. We echoed what Big A stated before. The younger officer finished his search of Big A. He ordered him to sit cross-legged on the side of the road, in the gravel. He came over and began to search me. He placed my wallet on the hood and the older officer searched through it. He looked at my driver's license and matched my picture to my face.

"So, what are you two doing in Texas?" he asked Tay-O and me. We told him about Nicole and explained why we were in Dallas. "You all aren't running some drugs or some money, are you?" he asked us.

"Nothing like that," Tay-O answered. "We're just giving a friend a ride. That's it."

The officer continued to rummage through my wallet and pulled out another ID. "What is this?" he exclaimed. "Is this what I think it is?" He held up my medical marijuana card.

"That's my medicinal card," I answered.

"Wow, I haven't seen one of these in person before," he said. "Would you look at that. I never thought I'd see the day." He just stood there staring at the ID, like I had brought it from the future. "Now you know that this ain't worth nothing in Texas," he added, "if we find some marijuana in that vehicle. This card won't do you any good." I nodded to confirm my understanding of state law.

The younger cop finished his search of my person. He then grabbed my and Big A's IDs and returned to the police car to run our information. The older officer made Tay-O and I sit alongside Big A on the gravel, with our hands behind our backs. I didn't understand why they were making us sit on the ground with our legs crossed. I assumed it was a psychological strategy that they learned in training. We were forced to sit there like some children as the officer stood over us.

The younger officer returned and placed our IDs on the hood of the police car. "You've got several priors," he said to Big A.

"So that's why you've been talking so much," the older officer chimed in. "You were hoping we wouldn't run your information."

"That's all in the past," Big A replied. "I have investments now. I'm trying to build toward my future. We wasn't doing nothing wrong." The older cop stood directly over him.

"Well you better hope we don't find anything in this vehicle, because a judge isn't going to look lightly at those priors," he told Big A.

"Tell us now if we're going to find anything when we search this car," the older officer continued. "I might take it easier on you all if you just tell the truth now." We informed him that the car was clean. He directed the younger officer to search Tay-O's vehicle. The police officers were moving at an extremely slow pace. While we sat and waited, I wondered what time it was, selfishly wishing that they would just hurry up because I had somewhere to be.

After the younger cop finished searching the passenger's side, the officers switched tasks. The older guy searched the trunk and then the driver's side. He poked around Tay-O's seat for a few minutes.

He finally emerged from the car. "What do we have here?" he said to us. "I found this under the driver's seat." He was holding something between his fingers. I couldn't even see what he was showing us. It was night and the headlights of the police cruiser were blinding me. I wasn't sure if he was actually holding anything at all.

"Looks like an Oxycodone pill to me." he said, "Who does this belong to?" We all denied ownership of the pill.

"I've never even seen an Oxycodone pill before," Tay-O said. "Where did you say you found that?"

"Right under your seat," the officer replied, "which means it's most likely yours."

"That's not mine, I swear," Tay-O answered. "I've never had anything like that in my car."

"Well, maybe your friend, who was sitting in the back there, hid it under your seat," the older officer theorized. "He's the one with a record. He's the one who keeps talking. Maybe he decided to try and put the blame on you."

"Whoa man, that's not mine!" Big A shouted. "I swear to god! I didn't have nothing on me."

"I wouldn't do that to you brother, I promise," Big A looked over at Tay-O and spoke. I sat there and shook my head in frustration. The officer's attempt to pit Tay-O against Big A felt underhanded and unnecessary.

"Maybe it's yours," the older cop said to me. "Maybe you tossed it down there when he wasn't looking."

"Come on man, that's not mine," I replied. "I have no idea where that

114

came from."

"Well, if no one is going to tell the truth," he said to all of us, "then I guess we're going to have to arrest all of you all." They proceeded to handcuff us as we remained seated on the side of the road. I started to get very nervous. The reality of the situation had just completely hit me. I was unclear on the severity of the accusation. I had heard stories about people spending months in jail on minor drug charges in Texas. My mind began to race. I was a thousand miles from home and possibly on my way to jail.

My plans for the night had suddenly become much less important. I figured whatever shot I had with Nikki's friend wasn't looking very good. Going to jail didn't seem like a good excuse for canceling our plans.

Big A began to plead his case again. "Look, I can't go to jail for this!" he insisted, "They probably gonna send me to prison. I didn't do nothing. Please! You gotta let me go." He hung his head.

"I'm begging you, officer," he continued. "I can't go to jail. Please don't do this to me." The older cop was pacing back-and-forth in front of us. He appeared to be considering Big A's request.

"Listen we're going to go over this one more time," the older officer informed us. "Is anyone going to take responsibility for the possession of this narcotic?" Again, the three of us denied ownership.

"Since you are the driver and it was found under your seat," the officer told Tay-O, "if you say that it's yours, then we will let these two go. Otherwise, you are all going to jail."

Tay-O shook his head and grimaced. He was stuck in a bad position. Claiming possession was admitting to guilt. That could come back to really hurt him later in the process. Telling the truth and not taking the fall meant that Big A and I were going to jail with him.

"Please man," Big A begged Tay-O, "I'll post your bond. I'll find you a lawyer." Tay-O hung his head and then looked up at the older officer.

"Alright man," he said, "I'll say it's mine." The two cops picked him up and placed him on his feet.

115

"So, you are telling me that this is your pill?" the older officer asked him. "Yes, it's my pill," Tay-O mumbled. The younger officer cuffed him and placed him in the backseat of their car.

"When they give you your phone call," Big A shouted to Tay-O, "Call me man. I'll come and get you brother. I ain't gonna forget what you did for us partner." Tay-O nodded his head as the officer closed the door.

"One of you can take possession of the vehicle with his consent," the older cop informed Big A and me, "otherwise, the vehicle will sit here and eventually get towed." I obviously offered to take Tay-O's car. The officer got Tay-O's consent and returned our belongings. I drove Big A to his parent's house. He wanted to stay there and wait for Tay-O's call. We sat out front for a minute.

"I can't believe they did that shit man!" Big A shouted. "Do you think they planted that pill in there?"

"If it was just sitting under the seat," I replied, "what took him so long to find it?"

"Them police wanted to take us to jail from the start," Big A said. "I didn't think that they was going to take it that far, though. I thought for sure that we was all getting locked up tonight. Tay-O saved our asses man!"

"A judge would have really sent you to prison for real, just because of your priors?" I asked him.

"Down here it's fucked up man," he replied. "You could have done something ten years ago, but they're going to dig all that shit up and act like you just did it yesterday. These judges are trying to give people the most time possible."

"That's crazy bro," I replied. "They ain't gonna give Tay-O jail time for this right?"

"Who knows man," Big A replied. "They might." Before going inside, Big A gave me his phone number and promised to call me once he heard something from Tay-O.

I headed back to Nikki's apartment. I was not looking forward to telling her what happened. She had a tendency to overreact to any form of drama. When I pulled into Nikki's apartment complex, I saw her friend's car parked in the lot. She was supposed to pick me up at 9 PM. I was only twenty minutes late, so I didn't feel like I messed her whole night up. I thought it wouldn't be cool to go out while Tay-O was locked up, but it was still early enough for her to make other plans. I felt like the opportunity to reschedule our date was still alive. Tay-O would have wanted me to go out, but he took one for the guys. I felt like it would be more respectful to the situation to lay low and see how everything played out.

I went upstairs and Nikki opened the door. "Where have you been?" she asked me, "I've been calling Tay-O and he's not picking his phone up! What the fuck? Where is he?" She went outside and looked around the parking lot.

"Come back inside," I told her. "I'll tell you what happened." I went into the kitchen and gave Nikki's friend a hug. I apologized for my tardiness. I went on to explain everything. Nikki received the information and remained uncharacteristically calm. She was being cool in front of her friend and I appreciated it.

"So, what should we do?" Nikki asked. "Should we go to the police station?" I let her know that Big A was going to handle the situation and we just needed to wait for him to call.

Nikki's friend was very understanding and didn't seem to mind the change in plans. The three of us hung out and waited for the call. A couple of hours went by and we still hadn't heard anything, so I called Big A. He was at the police station, waiting for them to release Tay-O. About an hour later, Big A and Tay-O came walking through the door.

Nikki jumped up to greet him. We hung out for a while and talked in the kitchen. It was late and Nikki's friend was getting tired. We didn't get to go out that night, but we were still able to spend some time together.

The following evening, Tay-O and I sat around talking. "They charged me with a misdemeanor possession," he told me. "I'm probably going to have to take a deal because there is no way to fight this shit!" He was nervous, because in Texas jail time was an actual possibility.

The reality of Tay-O's situation was eye opening. Both of us had dealt with false charges from the police before that night. We had both experienced first-hand the police planting or manufacturing evidence in order to drive up their arrest totals, but being from a liberal state, the consequences of police corruption could be tempered by the values of the judges.

We had dealt with the same old unjustified profiling at the hands of the police, but on the south side of Dallas, there was more at stake. The approach of the Dallas Police was new to me, but the racial targeting and the illegal tactics weren't. We were in a predominantly Black neighborhood, and the police did everything possible to manufacture an arrest. The combination of crooked police officers and conservative judges was frightening. I wondered how many of the hundreds of thousands of people locked up in Texas were arrested due to illegal police behavior.

I was scheduled to depart from Dallas in a couple of days. I wanted to make sure that I spent more time with Nikki's friend. We were connecting very quickly, and I ended up changing my flight to stay for a few more days. We decided that we needed to attempt the seemingly impossible challenge of a long-distance relationship.

Long story short, we made it work and we have been together ever since. That friend of Nikki's is now my wife and we have built a family together. I have always felt a debt to Tay-O for what he did that night. My entire life might have played out differently if all three of us had gone to jail.

Tay-O ended up taking a deal. He was sentenced to some home confinement and a year of probation. He was happy to not serve jail time, but his life had been upended for simply giving a friend a ride. The only thing he was guilty of was Driving While Black.

14

AFTERWORD

As I wrap this up, I feel the need to clearly restate what compelled me to share my stories. These stories are important because I have no stories of being harassed by the police except while with Black people. Many times, I have dealt with law enforcement, alone or with people who aren't Black, and never once have we dealt with illegal searches or violent police misconduct. It's not that the police never harass or even profile all kinds of people, but the level of racial and persistent targeting, and the extreme violence and violation of civil rights experienced by Black Americans at the hands of the police, is unique. "Driving While Black" exists as a slang term because of how common racial targeting is, just as Black Lives Matter exists as a movement because police have been operating as if they don't.

In my experience, many non-Blacks have a hard time being overtly critical of law enforcement, because they simply can't relate. Most of them do not have a list of stories involving police misconduct. I urge everybody to listen and trust other's stories of injustice at the hands of the police. Like most major social reforms in our history, it's going to take a lot of voices to create a change. Acknowledging the severity of racist policing, and the damage it causes to the lives of Black Americans, is a crucial first step toward making this issue a priority.

We need to make police reform a key political issue on which elections will be won or lost. From local government to the White House, we have to let them know that this matter must be dealt with immediately. The notion that politicians will find a remedy on their own is not something I would bet on. This is why the growing public discussion on police reform is so important, and why it must continue until we see real change.

One of the most important things we need to do is reexamine police tactics and decide who we, as civilians, want the police to be, not let them tell us who they are. We need to disregard how cop movies and TV shows justify rogue behavior. The police need to be held to the same societal standards as the rest of us. This issue will not be resolved until we have full transparency, and babysitters monitoring every move that law enforcement makes.

Many common police tactics need to be changed or eliminated, but there's one which has stuck with me the most, and that's when a traffic infraction turns into a search. If someone is guilty of a minor offense, they should be ticketed accordingly and that should be it. They shouldn't have to answer a bunch of questions and be victimized. If someone doesn't pay their property tax, the police don't come to their house and question them. The cops don't start searching their home unannounced. Why is a vehicle so different? The police should not be able to use an expired sticker as a clear path to violating people's rights.

Dramatic police reform, and a complete reimagining of the role of law enforcement in American society, is urgently needed. If all of these issues went away tomorrow, it would still be far too late. Too many lives have been lost and too many people's freedom has been unjustly taken away.